Understanding HIPAA

The Employer's Guide to Compliance

By

Michael Murphy; Mark Waterfill; Janet Braun

1stBooks – rev. 10/13/03

Notice To Purchasers Of This Book

Thank you for purchasing our book on HIPAA Compliance. Your purchase of this book entitles you to a HIPAA Training Program at no charge. The training program is available on CD, which can be sent to you directly by post or can be sent to you electronically via e-mail.

To order your FREE (no shipping or handling charges) training program please e-mail Laurie Cobian at: lcobian@pcsi-inc.com. In that e-mail provide her with the following information.

Your Name: _____

Address: _____

Phone Number: _____

E-mail Address _____

Please send training program ASAP

Via e-mail   [ ] yes [ ] no
Via US Mail [ ] yes [ ] no

When and where di d you purchase the HIPAA Compliance Book?

_____

_____

_____

_____

Thank you again for buying our book. You can expect your free training program within ten days.

Table of Content

Notice To Purchasers Of This Book..iii

Understanding HIPAA:..1

The Employer's Guide to Compliance..1

Part One: The History Of HIPAA Legislation............................ 1
Part Two: Definitions and Key TermsUsed In The HIPAA Privacy
        Rule.. 11
Part Three: Questions and Answers About "HIPAA" & The
        Privacy Rule.. 19
Part Four: Requirements and Exclusions.................................... 25
Part Five: Smart Compliance Strategies:................................... 33
Part Six: Employer Guidelines For Compliance With The Privacy
        Rule.. 45

Appendix.. 51

Certifications and Documents:.. 51
Sample Privacy Notice.. 55
First Sample Job Description... 62
Sample Policy, Authorization to Disclose Protected Health
        Information 75
Standards For Privacy Of Individually Identifiable Health
        Information [*45 Cfr Parts 160 And 164*] 78
Minimum Necessary [45 Cfr §§ 164.502(B), 164.514(D)].......... 96
Oral Communications [45 Cfr §§ 160.103, 164.501]................. 104
Business Associates [45 Cfr §§ 160.103, 164.502(E), 164.514(E)]
        110
Health-Related Communications And Marketing [45 Cfr §§
        164.501, 164.514(E)].. 117
Research [45 Cfr §§ 164.501, 164.508(F), 164.512(I)]................ 124
Research Use/Disclosure Without Authorization:...................... 125
Restrictions On Government Access To Health Information [45 Cfr
        §§ 160.300; 164.512(B); 164.512(F)].......................... 133

Index Of Key Terms 141

Premier Consulting Services incorporated®

One American Square, Suite 2300, Box 82008 Indianapolis, Indiana, 46282 317-632-4037 (Office) 317-946-2072 (Cell) 317-423-9079 (Fax)

At Premier Consulting Services *Inc*., ® we provide human resources consulting services to clients throughout the United States. We understand that in today's complex world of personnel – human resources management, with ever increasing compliance issues pressing on employers, that there is a need for reliable, effective, human resources management services. Our goal at PCS*i*® is to provide those services in a professional manner and a reasonable price.

Too often HR Consultants speak a language only they understand. When they are done talking the client is left confused and uncertain as to what will happen, when, and why. Our consultants do not use that approach. They are professional, personable, and approachable. At PCS*i*® we listen carefully, very carefully, to the human resources -- personnel needs of the client and then tailor our services to meet those needs. We explain carefully what we will do, how we will do it and what it will cost. Our consultants are well trained in all aspects of HR management. They are individuals with many years of hands on HR experience. They know and appreciate the value of effective "HR" and they understand that each client has a business to run, so their advice and suggestions must be practical and useful.

At PCS*i*® we value our clients, their time, their needs, and we want them to be comfortable with us at all levels. Primarily we want them to feel absolutely free to call on us at any time for HR assistance. That is what we are here for and we love what we do.

Understanding HIPAA: The Employer's Guide to Compliance

Part One: The History Of HIPAA Legislation

 What Is HIPAA?

> **Editor's Note:** A little history of HIPAA: The Health Insurance Portability and Accountability Act (**HIPAA**) of 1996, was passed by Congress in order to increase access to, and the efficiency of, the healthcare system in the United States. Some provisions of the bill required the Department of Health and Human Services (HHS), to adopt national standards for electronic healthcare transactions to make the system more efficient. The Congress became concerned that electronic technology might erode personal privacy, particularly privacy of health care information. To prevent this, Congress incorporated into HIPAA provisions that mandated federal privacy protection for individually identifiable health, information or **Private Health Information**. This became known as "The Privacy Rule."

"HIPAA" was originally known as the Kennedy-Kassebaum Act. HIPAA was passed, in part, to protect the privacy and security of health information and to set up a uniform standard for processing an individual's electronic health data between organizations. HIPAA and its accompanying regulations establish a national framework providing health care users a base level of privacy and security in connection with their medical care. Another purpose of HIPAA is to force employer group health plans and health providers, to improve the efficiency and effectiveness of health care delivery by building on efforts already underway by states, health systems, and individual organizations.

1

As the Congress was drafting HIPAA it became clear from testimony that privacy safeguards be built into HIPAA to protect the personal nature of health information. An individual's health information contains intimate details about the individual's mental and physical health. These records many times contain additional information about a person's social behaviors, personal relationships, and financial status. Unwarranted and un-necessary disclosures of this information could, and has, lead to discrimination against persons, loss of trust in medical providers, and resulted in failure to seek medical treatment or to disclose important information to health care professionals.

It is amazing how much very personal and highly private information about a person is spread around in the process of providing medical treatment. Prior to HIPAA, totally identifiable, individual health information was routinely shared with consulting physicians, managed care organizations, health/life insurance companies, employers with self-insured plans, pharmacies, benefit managers, and clinical laboratories with the person affected exercising very little control over this information. Many times this included patient information about their marital status, age, gender, race, number of children, occupation, hobbies, employment status, income level, and credit history!

Who Knows What About You? A Quiz? (Pre-HIPAA)

**T.   F.   **All medical information is confidential and is shared on a need to know basis.

**T.   F.   **Medical professionals and others take extraordinary measures to protect access to all medical information.

**T.   F.   **As the patient I am consulted before my medical information is shared.

The answer to the three statements above is false for all three.

The Preamble to the Final HIPAA Privacy Rule states "an average 150 people 'from nursing staff to x-ray technicians, to billing clerks' have access to a patient's medical records. . . no [consistently applied] laws govern who these people are, what information they are able to see, and what they are and are not allowed to do with that information once they have… it."

The Congress noted several breaches of security that greatly influenced its decision making process as regards HIPAA.

In one state a health care system unintentionally posted private health information about thousands of patients on the Internet. In another instance the health insurance claims forms of thousands of persons fell out of a truck on its way to a recycling center. A patient in a large metropolitan hospital accidentally discovered that her medical record had been read by more than 200 of the hospital's employees. Out west a woman purchased a used computer and discovered that the computer still contained the prescription records of the customers of the pharmacy that had previously owned the computer. The intact data base included names, addresses, social security numbers, and a list of all the medicines the customers had purchased. In another instance a person working at a financial institution also sat on a county health board. In this capacity that person gained access to private health information identifying several customers of the institution as having cancer and acting on that information called in their mortgages. In one hospital, a member of the medical staff was diagnosed with HIV resulting in suspension of surgical privileges. A long-term employee of the FBI was placed on administrative leave when his pharmacy released information revealing his treatment for depression.

The HIPAA Privacy Rule was published by the U.S. Department of Health and Human Services (HHS) on December 28, 2000. Modifications were adopted in August 2002. The rule provides comprehensive federal protection for the privacy of health information. HHS has stated that the Privacy Rule, as modified, is carefully balanced to provide strong privacy protections that do not interfere with patient access to, or the quality of, healthcare delivery.

The coverage of the HIPAA Privacy Rule is limited to three types of entities over which HHS has authority under HIPAA. These are:
1.   Health plans;
2.   Healthcare clearinghouses; and
3.   Healthcare providers who conduct certain healthcare transactions electronically.

The date for compliance with these regulations is April 14, 2003, (April 14, 2004, for small health plans). Under these regulations, covered entities must develop and implement standards to protect and guard against the misuse of individually identifiable health information, (PHI). To put "teeth" in this requirement, the privacy Rule provides for civil and/or criminal penalties for failure to implement these standards in a timely manner.

Essentially, the Privacy Rule establishes federal protections for the privacy of protected health information (PHI).

Editor's Note: 1). HIPAA does not replace any other law that grants greater privacy protections. 2). Covered entities are free to retain or adopt more protective policies or practices.	**Editor's Note:** The Privacy Rule regulates employers only in their role as sponsors of group health plans, as health insurers or HMOs, and (perhaps) as healthcare providers.

The Basics of The Privacy Rule

       The HIPAA Privacy Rule…

1.   Creates federal standards to protect PHI.
2.   Gives patients, (therefore your employees) more control over their health information, (PHI).
3.   Sets limits on the use and release of health records, (PHI).

4.	Establishes safe guards that providers and health plans must implement to protect the privacy of health information, (PHI).

5.	Provides that a covered entity may not use or disclose an individual's healthcare information, (PHI) without permission except for treatment, payment, or healthcare operations. (Consent versus Authorization).

6.	Enables and permits that individuals may find out how their healthcare information may be used **and** if unnecessary or unlawful disclosures of their information have been made.

7.	In a general sense The Privacy Rule limits the release of information to the minimum amount reasonably needed for the purpose of the disclosure.

8.	Gives patients, and your employees the right to access and examine a copy of their own health records **and** request corrections.

9.	Permits persons to exercise reasonable and necessary control over certain uses of, and/or disclosures about, their health care information, (PHI).

The Privacy Rule will require that healthcare providers, or health plans…

1.	Notify patients, (your employees) of their privacy rights and how such information can be used.

2.	Develop and implement privacy procedures for physician practices, hospitals, or insurance plans that are covered by the rule.

3.	Requires employers to train their employees so that the employees understand their rights under the privacy rule and that employees with necessary access to PHI understand their obligations to maintain the privacy of this information.

4.	Requires an employer to designate an individual to be responsible for seeing that privacy procedures in accordance with HIPAA requirements are adopted and followed.

> **Editor's Note:** This requirement includes developing new position descriptions for the "Privacy Officer" and the "Contact Person."

5.   Secure patient, (your employees) records containing individually identifiable health information (PHI) so they are not accessible to those who do not need them.

Are Employers Covered Under HIPAA?

In HIPAA, Congress did not specifically provide HHS with authority to regulate employers under the Privacy Rule. HIPAA does, however, give HHS the authority to regulate health plans. Since employers may sponsor a group health plan that is a covered entity under the rule, the employer (that is, "plan sponsor") must make sure that all requirements of the Privacy Rule are met.

Employers, Only as Employers: Are they covered entities?

HHS would say, in general employers are not covered entities. However, employers are effected by the Privacy Rule if they are a sponsor of a group health plan. Therefore, if you are providing group health coverage under a partially or fully self-funded plan you may be considered as a covered entity, **or,** if you have access to PHI about your employees you are a covered entity.

> **Editor's Note:** Employers do have specific requirements under HIPAA, which, will be discussed, at length, below.

Timelines for Compliance

The first compliance date for the HIPAA Privacy Rule is April 14, 2003. This compliance date applies to all covered entities except small health plans, (A small health plan is defined as a plan with annual receipts of $5 million or less. The HHS Office of Civil Rights, which is responsible for enforcement of the Privacy Rule, has issued guidance on how plans are to calculate annual receipts). Small Health Plans have until April 14, 2004.

> **Editor's Note:** The regulations contain procedures for determining small plan status for plans such as ERISA compliant group health plans that are exempt from filing federal income tax returns and plans that do file an income tax return.

How to Determine Your Annual Receipts

1. Health plans that do not report receipts to the Internal Revenue Service (IRS) are required to use equivalency or proxy methods for determining annual receipts.
2. Fully insured health plans must use the amount of total premiums paid for health insurance benefits during the plan's last full fiscal year.
3. Self-insured plans, both funded and non-funded, are required to use the total amount paid for:
   a. Healthcare claims by the employer;
   b. The plan sponsor; or
   c. The benefit fund on behalf of the plan during the plan's last full fiscal year.
4. Plans that provide health benefits through a mix of purchased insurance and self-insurance are instructed

Michael Murphy; Mark Waterfill; Janet Braun

to combine the income generated from the two measures to determine their total annual receipts.

Editor's Note: Partially self-insured plans, which have stop-loss insurance, are not to include the cost of the premiums for stop-loss coverage for health insurance benefits when calculating their total receipts.

Business Associate Contracts

"Business Associates" is the term used to refer to service providers, such as third-party administrators, actuaries, or others. It includes:

1. Any entity who(m) receives individually identifiable health information from the covered entity;
2. Creates – stores individually identifiable health information; or
3. Discloses individually identifiable health information in the course of providing services on behalf of the covered entity.

 The Privacy Rule requires:

1. New written provisions in the agreements that covered entities have with business associates;
2. New written contracts must include provisions to ensure that the privacy of health information is protected even though the business associates are not, or may not, be directly regulated by the Privacy Rule.

 Deadlines For New Contracts

Covered entities (other than small health plans) which, had an existing contract with a business associate prior to October 15, 2002, are:

1. Permitted to continue to operate under that contract for an additional year beyond the April 14, 2003, compliance date;
2. Provided the contract is not renewed or modified prior to April 14, 2003.
3. This transition period applies only to written contracts or agreements;
    a. Existing oral contracts or other arrangements are not eligible for the transition period.
    b. Covered entities with contracts that qualify are permitted to continue to operate under those contracts with their business associates until April 14, 2004; or

c. Until the contract is renewed or modified, whichever is sooner even though the contract may not comply with the requirements of the Privacy Rule.

> **Editor's Note:** Regardless of the above limitations and considerations, a covered entity, may only make disclosures of protected health information to the business associate. No other information concerning the individual may be disclosed.

Part Two: Definitions and Key Terms
Used In The HIPAA Privacy Rule

Term	Definition
HHS	The abbreviation for the Department of Health and Human Services. This is the federal entity responsible for enforcing HIPAA requirements.
Protected Health Information (PHI) **See Pages 65 and 78 for additional information on PHI**	Health information, which is individually identifiable, that is transmitted either by electronic means, **or** maintained in an electronic form, **or** transmitted **or** maintained in any other form or medium. **Editor's Note:** Error on the safe side. PHI includes almost **ALL** individually identifiable information. The definition of PHI is very broad and covers almost all health information that could be reasonably associated with a particular individual, **and** is in the possession of a covered entity.
Health Information	Information that relates to: 1. The past, present, or future physical or mental health or condition of an individual; 2. The provision of health care to an individual; or 3. The past, present, or future payment for provision of health care to an individual.
Individually Identifiable Health Information	Health information (including demographic information such as age, race, gender) created or received by a covered entity, which identifies the individual or, includes information, which could be used to identify the individual.

Treatment; Payment; Health Care Operations. TPO	A patient's personal health information needed to carry out treatment, payment, or health care operations (TPO). Before HIPAA, many health care providers, for professional or ethical reasons, routinely obtained a patient's consent for disclosure of information to insurance companies or for other purposes. The Privacy Rule establishes a uniform standard for health care providers to use in order to obtain their patients' consent for uses and disclosures of health information about the patient needed to carry out Treatment, Payment or health care Operations. (TPO)
Covered Entities	Health care providers, health plans, and health care clearing houses. Employers are not covered entities unless they are also one of the above entities.
Providers	A healthcare facility, a provider of medical or health services, and/or any other person or organization who furnishes, bills, or is paid for health care in the usual and customary course of operating its business.
Authorization	A written form signed by the employee or patient, providing written documentation of their "consent" to allow covered entities access to their PHI.
Treatment	The provision, coordination, or management of healthcare and related services by providers, including the coordination or management by a provider with a third party; consultation between providers relating to a patient; or referrals from one healthcare provider to another.
Group Health Plans Encompassed By	Medical Plans; Dental Plans; Vision Plans; Prescription Drug Plans; Employee Assistance Plans; Long-Term Care Plans; and

The Privacy Rule	Health Based Flexible Spending Accounts.
Consent	A patient's written consent (by use of an authorization form) is required before a covered health care provider that has a direct treatment relationship with the patient may use or disclose protected health information (PHI) for purposes of TPO. Uses and disclosures for TPO may be permitted without prior consent in an emergency, when a provider is required by law to treat the individual, or when there are substantial communication barriers. Health care providers that have indirect treatment relationships with patients (such as laboratories that only interact with physicians and not patients), health plans, and health care clearinghouses may use and disclose PHI for purposes of TPO without obtaining a patient's consent. The rule permits such entities to obtain consent, if they choose. If a patient refuses to consent to the use or disclosure of their PHI to carry out TPO, the health care provider may refuse to treat the patient. A patient's written consent need only be obtained by a provider one time.
Clearing House	A public or private entity, including a billing service; a company that prices or re-prices services; a community health management information system; a community health information system; and a "value-added" network and switcher, that performs either of the following functions: (1) Processes health information received from another entity in a nonstandard format or containing nonstandard data content into standard elements or standard transaction. (2) Receives a standard transaction from another entity and processes or facilitates the

	processing of health information into nonstandard format or nonstandard data content for the receiving entity.
Group Health Plans	An ERISA compliant employee benefit welfare plan that provides medical care whether it is fully insured or self-insured. Does not include an employer-administered plan that has fewer than 50 participants.
Health Plans: In General	Individual or group plans that pay the cost of medical care including: Group health plans; Health insurance issuers; HMOs; Medicare (Parts A or B); Medicaid; issuer of a Medicare supplemental policy; issuer of a long-term care policy (unless it is a nursing home fixed indemnity policy); a multiple or multi-employer health benefit plan; Federal programs that provide health benefits; State child health benefit programs; State high-risk pools; or any other individual or group plan, or combination of individual or group plans, that provides or pays for the cost of medical care.
Payment	Activities of a health plan to obtain premiums or to provide coverage and benefits under the health plan. It also encompasses actions taken by a provider or plan to obtain or provide reimbursement for the provision of health care.
Included In Payment	Eligibility determinations (including coordination of benefits or the determination of cost sharing amounts), and adjudication or subrogation of health benefit claims. Billing, claims management, collection activities, obtaining payment under a contract for reinsurance (including stop-loss insurance and excess of loss insurance), and related healthcare data processing. Risk assessments.

Included In Payment	Medical necessity and similar determinations. Utilization review activities, including pre-certification and preauthorization of services, concurrent and retrospective review of services. Disclosure to consumer reporting agencies of any of the following PHI relating to collection of premiums or reimbursement: Name and address; Date of birth; Social Security number; Payment history; Account number; or name and address of the healthcare provider.
Healthcare Operations	The following activities of a covered entity that relate to a covered function: Quality assessment and improvement including activities such as outcomes evaluation and development of clinical guidelines: population-based activities for improving health or reducing healthcare costs, protocol development, case management and care coordination, contacting of healthcare providers and patients with information about treatment alternatives. Reviewing healthcare personnel competence and qualifications. Reviewing practitioner and provider performance. Reviewing health plan performance. Conducting training programs. Underwriting, premium rating, and other activities for the creation, renewal, or replacement of a health insurance contract or health benefits (including stop-loss insurance and excess of loss insurance). Conducting or arranging for medical review, legal services, and auditing functions including fraud and abuse detection and compliance programs.

Healthcare Operations Continued:	Business planning and development such as conducting cost-management and planning-related analyses (*including formulary development and administration, development or improvement of methods of payment, or coverage policies*). Business management and general administrative activities including: *Management activities for complying with the HIPAA Privacy Rule. Customer service, including the preparation of data analyses for policyholders, plan sponsors, or other customers. Resolution of internal grievances. The sale, transfer, merger, or consolidation of all or part of the covered entity with another covered entity. Creating identified health information or a limited data set and fundraising for the benefit of the covered entity.*
An Exception.	**Editor's Note:** If a health plan receives PHI for underwriting, premium rating, or other activities relating to the creation, renewal, or replacement of a contract of health insurance or health benefits, and if such health insurance or health benefits are not placed with the health plan, that health plan may not use or disclose the PHI for any other purpose except when required by law.
Standard Transactions	The transmission of information between two parties to carry out financial or administrative activities related to health care. Includes: _ Health care claims or equivalent information; _ Health care payment and remittance advice; _ Coordination of benefits; _ Health care claim status;

Standard Transactions	_ Enrollment and/or de-enrollment in a health plan; _ Eligibility for a health plan; _ Health plan premium payments; _ Referral certification and authorization; _ First report of injury; and _ Health claims attachments.
The General Rule Regarding Employers	As an employer if your group health plan is fully insured, it is the insurance company that needs to bring the plan into compliance with the Privacy Rule under HIPAA. If, the employer's group health plan is fully or partially self-funded, it is the obligation of the employer to assure that the plan complies with the Privacy Rule. **Generally, employers maintain at least one self-funded group health plan. Often times this self-funded plan is a health based flexible spending account.**
Exceptions To The General Rule	Under HIPAA, the Privacy Rule does not cover every plan that could possibly involve health information. **The following plans are not covered:** workers' compensation; disability plans which provide only income; life insurance plans; and sick leave accumulation plans.
Personal Representative Under the Rule you must verify a personal representative's authority in the same way that they are required	A personal representative is a designated individual, sometimes with "Power of Attorney" who has the authority to act for another. In these situations you must provide the employee's personal representative with an accounting of disclosures and provide the personal representative access to the individual's PHI if requested. A personal representative may also authorize disclosures

to verify the identity of any person requesting access to PHI. Remember: Under the Rule you must verify a personal representative's authority in the same way that they are required to verify the identity of any person requesting access to PHI.	of the individual PHI. The degree to which an individual personal representative has authority to act for another under the Privacy Rule is based on his or her authority to make healthcare decisions for the individual. When the person has broad authority to act on the behalf of a living individual in making decisions related to health care, such as a parent with respect to a minor child the covered entity must treat the personal representative as the individual for all purposes. Where the authority to act for the individual is limited or specific to particular healthcare decisions, the personal representative is limited to that area. State or other law determines who is authorized to act on an individual's behalf. The Privacy Rule does not address how personal representatives should be identified. Covered entities should continue to identify personal representatives in the same way they have in the past. However, under the Rule, you must verify a personal representative's authority in the same way that they are required to verify the identity of any person requesting access to PHI.

Part Three: Questions and Answers About "HIPAA" & The Privacy Rule

The Privacy Rule created a federal requirement that most doctors, hospitals, or other health care providers obtain a patient's written consent before using or disclosing the patient's personal health information to carry out treatment, payment, or health care operations. The Privacy Rule establishes a uniform standard for certain health care providers to obtain their patients' consent for uses and disclosures of health information about the patient to carry out TPO. In order to assure that you fully understand the issue of consent we have researched and answered the following questions.

Q: What is "consent" under the Privacy Rule?

A: "Consent" is a general document that gives health care providers, having a direct treatment relationship with a patient, permission to use and disclose all PHI for TPO. It gives permission only to that provider. Health care providers **may condition the provision of treatment on the individual providing this consent**. One "consent" may cover all uses and disclosures for TPO by that provider, indefinitely. A "consent" need not specify the particular information to be used or disclosed, nor the recipients of disclosed information. Only doctors or other health care providers with a direct treatment relationship with a patient are required to obtain consent.

Q. What is a "direct treatment provider?"

A. In general a "direct treatment provider" is one that treats a patient directly, rather than based on the orders of another provider, and/or provides health care services or test results directly to patients. Other health care providers, health plans, and health care clearinghouses may use or disclose information for TPO without consent, or may choose to obtain a consent.

19

Michael Murphy; Mark Waterfill; Janet Braun

Q: What is "authorization" under the Privacy Rule?

A: An authorization is a customized document that gives covered entities permission to use specified PHI for specified purposes, which are generally other than TPO, or to disclose PHI to a third party specified by the individual. **Covered entities may not condition treatment** or coverage on the individual providing an authorization. An authorization is more detailed and specific than a "consent."

a.   It covers only the uses and disclosures and only the PHI stipulated in the authorization.

b.   It has an expiration date; and, in some cases, it also states the purpose for which the information may be used or disclosed.

An authorization is required for use and disclosure of PHI not otherwise allowed by the rule. In general, this means an authorization is required for purposes that are not part of TPO. All covered entities, not just direct treatment providers, must obtain an authorization to use or disclose PHI for these purposes.

Q.   What are examples of when an authorization would be required?

A.   For example, a covered entity would need an authorization from individuals to sell a patient mailing list, to disclose information to an employer for employment decisions, or to disclose information for eligibility for life insurance. A covered entity will never need to obtain both an individual's consent and authorization for a single use or disclosure. However, a provider may have to obtain consent and authorization from the same patient for different uses or disclosures. For example, an obstetrician may, under the consent obtained from the patient, send an appointment reminder to the patient, but would need authorization from the patient to send her name and address to a company marketing a diaper service.

Q.   When is" consent" required?

A.   Consent is required before a covered health care provider that has a direct treatment relationship with the patient may use or disclose protected health information (PHI) for purposes of TPO. However, uses and disclosures of PHI may be permitted, without prior consent, under certain circumstances.

a.   It is an emergency;
b.   The provider is required by law to treat the individual; or
c.   There are substantial communication barriers.

Q.   Is there ever a time when "consent" is not required?

A.   Health care providers that have indirect treatment relationships with patients (such as laboratories that only interact with physicians and not patients), health plans, and health care clearinghouses may use and disclose PHI for purposes of TPO without obtaining a patient's consent. However, the rule permits such entities to obtain consent, if they choose. If a patient refuses to consent to the use or disclosure of their PHI to carry out TPO, the health care provider may refuse to treat the patient.

Q.   Does "consent" have to be given for each individual event?

A.   No. A patient's written consent need only be obtained by a provider one time.

Q.   How is consent to disclose PHI given?

A.   Consent is given by an individual through the use of a "Consent Form." The form is usually provided by the covered entity. If a covered entity obtains "consent" and receives an "authorization" to disclose PHI for TPO, the covered entity may disclose information only in accordance with the more restrictive document, unless the covered entity resolves the conflict with the individual.

Michael Murphy; Mark Waterfill; Janet Braun

Q.   What are my rights as an individual regarding consent?

A.   The Privacy rule extends numerous rights to individuals concerning control over their PHI.

a.   An individual may revoke consent, but it must be done in writing;

b.   An individual may request additional restrictions on uses or disclosures of their PHI for purposes of TPO. The covered entity is bound by any restriction to which it agrees; and

c.   An individual must be given a notice of the covered entity's privacy practices and may review that notice prior to signing a consent.

Q.   How long is "consent" valid?

A.   A covered entity must retain the signed consent for 6 years from the date it was last in effect. The Privacy Rule does not dictate the form in which these consents are to be retained by the covered entity.

Q.   Are health plans or clearinghouses required to obtain an individual's consent to use or disclose PHI to carry out TPO?

A: No. Health plans and clearinghouses may use and disclose PHI for these purposes without obtaining consent. However, these entities are permitted to obtain consent. If they choose to seek individual consent for these uses and disclosures, the consent must meet the standards, requirements, and implementation specifications for consents set forth under the Privacy Rule.

Q: Can direct treatment providers, such as a specialist or hospital, to whom a patient is referred for the first time, use PHI to set up appointments or schedule surgery or other procedures before obtaining the patient's written consent?

A: No. The Privacy Rule, currently does not permit uses of PHI prior to obtaining the patient's written consent for TPO.

Q: Does the consent requirement restrict the ability of providers to consult with other providers about a patient's condition?

A: No. A provider with a direct treatment relationship with a patient would have to have initially obtained consent to use that patient's health information for treatment purposes. Consulting with another health care provider about the patient's case falls within the definition of "treatment" and is permitted. If the provider being consulted does not otherwise have a direct treatment relationship with the patient, that provider does not need to obtain the patient's consent to engage in the consultation.

Q: Can a pharmacist use PHI to fill a prescription that was telephoned in by a patient's physician if the patient is a new patient to the pharmacy and has not yet provided written consent to the pharmacy?

A: No. The Privacy Rule currently does not permit this activity without prior patient consent.

Q: Does a pharmacist have to obtain "consent" under the Privacy Rule in order to provide advice about over-the-counter medicines to customers?

A: No. A pharmacist may provide advice about over-the-counter medicines without obtaining the customers' prior consent, provided that the pharmacist does not create or keep a record of any PHI. In this case, the only interaction or disclosure of information is a conversation between the pharmacist and the customer. The pharmacist may disclose PHI about the customer to the customer without obtaining his or her consent but may not otherwise use or disclose that information.

Q: Can a patient have a friend or family member pick up a prescription for her?

A: **Yes.** A pharmacist may use professional judgment and experience with common practice to make reasonable inferences of the patient's best interest in allowing a person, other than the patient, to pick up a prescription. For example, the fact that a relative or friend arrives at a pharmacy and asks to pick up a specific prescription for an individual effectively verifies that he or she is involved in the individual's care, and the rule allows the pharmacist to give the filled prescription to the relative or friend. The individual does not need to provide the pharmacist with the names of such persons in advance.

Q: How does the requirement for "consent" apply to "emergency treatment situations?"

A: Health care providers must exercise their professional judgment to determine whether obtaining a "consent" would interfere with the timely delivery of necessary health care. If, based on professional judgment, a provider reasonably believes at the time the patient presents for treatment that a delay involved in obtaining the patient's consent to use or disclose information would compromise the patient's care, the provider may use or disclose PHI that was obtained during the emergency treatment, without prior consent, to carry out TPO. **However,** the provider must attempt to obtain consent as soon as reasonably practicable after the provision of treatment. If the provider is able to obtain the patient's consent to use or disclose information before providing care, without compromising the patient's care, the Privacy Rule requires the provider to do so.

Q: How does the Privacy Rule interact with requirements under Title VI of the Civil Rights Act of 1964 or the Americans with Disabilities Act?

A: Entities that are covered by these statutes must continue to meet the requirements of the statutes. The Privacy Rule works in conjunction with these laws to remove impediments to access to necessary health care for all individuals.

Part Four: Requirements and Exclusions

1.   Employment Records Held by a Covered Entity.

Health information that a covered entity such as a hospital or other provider has about its employees in its employment records is not PHI. However, health information that the hospital has created or received about an employee while the employee is a patient of the provider is PHI. Also, health information that the hospital's health plan has created or received about an employee is PHI.

> **Editor's Note:** Remember that under the ADA and the FMLA medical information about employees of which the employer has knowledge is confidential.

2.   Exclusions from Coverage as Health Plans.   The following benefit plans are not covered by the Privacy Rule:

- Accident insurance.
- Workers' compensation insurance.
- Disability income insurance.
- Liability insurance including general liability insurance, supplemental liability insurance and automobile liability insurance.
- Automobile insurance, which pays for medical costs.
- Credit insurance.
- Insurance coverage for on-site medical clinics.
- Insurance coverage under which benefits for medical care are secondary or incidental to the reason for the insurance benefits.

> **Editor's Note:** The above are not "Health Plans." Health information that these plans have, use or disclose is not PHI and is **not** covered by the Privacy Rule.

The Use and Disclosure of PHI Permitted Under the Rule

 3.   May Disclose:

A covered entity may disclose PHI:

- With or without authorization to comply with workers' compensation insurance requirements;
- With or without authorization if required by law;
- For any event that is a permitted/required disclosure, **BUT**, minimum safeguards must be followed;
- For treatment, payment, or other healthcare operations;
- To the individual who's PHI is involved or to his/her designated representative; or
- Because of a valid authorization.

 4.   Required to Disclose:

- PHI must be disclosed to the person who the PHI is about when requested.
- During a compliance investigation conducted by a policing agency. For example during an OSHA audit providing information as to the type and frequency of on the job injuries or answering questions about a specific injury under investigation.

 5.   Requirement for the Authorization to be Valid:

Unless noted above under required to disclose, a covered **entity may not** use or disclose PHI without a valid authorization. With a valid authorization the use or disclosure of PHI must be consistent with the authorization. To be valid the authorization must contain the following minimum required elements:

- A readable and understandable description of the information to be disclosed.
- Identification of who is authorized to make the requested use or disclosure.
- Other specific identification to which the covered entity may make the disclosure.
- Description of each purpose of the requested use or disclosure.

> **Editor's Note:** Generally, the statement "at the request of the individual" is a sufficient description of the purpose when an individual initiates the authorization.

- An expiration date.
- Signature of the individual granting the authorization and date.

> **Editor's Note:** An example of an authorization is reproduced in the Appendix.

 6.   Revoking Authorization:

An individual employee who has granted authorization may revoke that authorization, for any reason, and at any time. To be binding revoking an authorization must be done in writing. However, if the authorization was obtained as a condition of obtaining insurance coverage and the insurer has the legal right to contest a claim under the policy it cannot be revoked until that issue is resolved.

 7.   Retaining Authorizations:

Properly completed authorizations must be retained for six years!!

8. Notice to the Individual of Their Rights When Granting An Authorization:

At a minimum the authorization must include all of the following.

- Authorization by the employee to the use and disclosure of my individually identifiable health information as described below.

- A statement such as the following: I understand that signing this Authorization is voluntary and that if I refuse to sign this form it will not prevent receipt of health care or eligibility for benefits under a health plan;

- I understand that I am entitled to receive a copy of this form upon signing it;

- I understand that if the organization or individual authorized to receive the information is not a health plan or health care provider, the released information may no longer be protected by federal privacy regulations;

- I understand that I have a right to revoke this Authorization. To do so it must be done in writing and delivered to the address below. I also understand that the revocation applies to uses and disclosures made after the revocation is made.

- Finally, a signed copy of an authorization requested by the covered entity must be provided to the individual.

9. Authorization for More Than One Purpose:

In most circumstances, authorizations for different purposes may be combined. However, an authorization that conditions the provisions of treatment, payment, enrollment in the health plan, or eligibility for benefits on its provision **may** **not** be combined with another authorization.

10.   Routine Disclosures:

A covered entity may presume in the following circumstances that the requested disclosure is the minimum necessary for the stated purpose:

1.   When making permitted disclosures to public officials, if the public official represents that the information requested is the minimum necessary for the stated purpose.

2.   The information is requested by another covered entity.

3.   The information is requested by a professional who is a member of its workforce or is a business associate of the covered entity to provide professional services to the covered entity, if the professional represents that the information requested is the minimum necessary for the stated purpose(s).

4.   Documentation that complies with the specified requirements has been provided by a person requesting the information for research purposes.

5.   A covered entity must also limit any request it makes for PHI from another covered entity to that which is reasonably necessary to accomplish the purpose for which the request is made.

6.   A policy or procedure may be implemented for routine and recurring requests.

11.   Non-routine Disclosures:

In the event a request for disclosure of PHI is not of a routine nature then it is classified as a non-routine disclosure. Before making a non-routine disclosure the covered entity must develop guidelines or establish criteria which are designed to limit the request for PHI to the information reasonably necessary to accomplish the purpose for which the request is made. Also the covered entity must review requests for non-routine disclosure on an individual basis to be sure they follow the guidelines established.

Editor's Note: The Privacy Rule requires that covered entities (read employers here) make reasonable efforts to limit access to PHI to those in the workforce that need access because of their job responsibilities. You are not required to completely restructure existing workflow systems, including redesigning office spaces and upgrading computer systems. That would be unreasonable. However, covered entities may need to make certain adjustments to their facilities to establish control over PHI and restrict access to it. This could include segregating the information; placing it in locking file cabinets; establishing records rooms, protecting by password or computer security programs.

Required Actions On The Part Of Covered Entities, (Employers)

1.   Handling Complaints:

The Privacy Policy along with any accompanying procedure establishes how and to whom individuals make complaints concerning policies or compliance with the Privacy Rule. Also, the policy must provide a method of documenting complaints received and any disposition.

2.   Penalties:

A covered entity, (employer) has to develop and apply appropriate penalties and discipline against members of the workforce who violate the Privacy Rule and the policy. Also, the policy must provide a method of documenting penalties or disciplinary actions.

Editor's Note: In the event the person violating the policy is engaged in whistle blowing activity, that would be protected and penalties and/or discipline would not be used against the "whistleblower" employee.

---

3.   Make Whole Remedies or Mitigation:

In the event that any harm is done to an individual that is known about, from the use or disclosure of PHI in violation of the Privacy Rule, the covered entity (employer) is required to mitigate that damage to the extent possible.

4.   Non-Retaliation or Intimidation:

The law specifically prohibits acts of intimidation; making threats; using coercion; discriminating against; or taking any action in retaliation against a person or employee for exercising their rights under HIPAA. Examples of actions employees might take include: filing complaints; providing testimony, assisting, or participating in an investigation; or compliance review; or proceeding, or hearing, or other enforcement procedure; **and/or** opposing any action unlawful under the Privacy Rule. Additionally you may not require individuals to waive their rights under HIPAA as a condition of treatment, payment, or enrollment in a health plan, or to be
eligible for such benefits.

> **Editor's Note:**   The prohibition against retaliatory action applies even if the person is mistaken but is acting in good faith on the belief that some action you have taken is a violation under HIPAA.

Part Five: Smart Compliance Strategies:

Protecting The Privacy of PHI and the Employee by use of Administrative; Technical; and Physical safeguards.

A covered entity (the employer) must have in place appropriate safeguards to protect the privacy of PHI. HHS recognizes three types of safeguards: administrative; technical; and physical. You must reasonably safeguard PHI from any intentional or unintentional use or disclosure, which would be a violation of the Privacy Rule. Additionally you must reasonably safeguard PHI to limit incidental uses or disclosures made pursuant to an otherwise permitted or required use or disclosure. There is no requirement to implement egregious or unreasonable safeguards in order to prevent incidental exposures.

Keeping Track of Disclosures:

A.   **What You Should Do.**

B.   **What You Should Not Do.**

C.   **What You Have To Do.**

Time Frame: As stated above, an authorization must be kept for six years. This means an individual employee has a right to receive an accounting of disclosure of their PHI made by a covered entity going back for six years. This accounting for disclosures includes telling of disclosures to or by a business associate or another employee.

Time Allowed to Comply: A covered entity must provide the information requested no later than 60 days after receipt of a request.

Accounting Charges: The first accounting requested by an individual in any 12-month period must be made without charge. A reasonable fee may be charged for each subsequent request by the same individual within a 12-month period. You have to tell them this.

Documentation Of The Accounting Process....
Six Years and Counting:
Document the accounting by retaining the following information for six years.
All information required to be included in an accounting;
  Any written accounting that is provided to the individual; and
The title of the persons or offices responsible for receiving and responding to requests for an accounting.

The accounting does not have to include the following:
Disclosures to carry out treatment, payment, and healthcare operations;
Disclosures to individuals of their own PHI at their own request;
Disclosures related to or necessary because of another permitted disclosure;
Disclosures made in compliance with an authorization
Disclosures for a facility directory or to persons involved in providing care; and/or
Disclosures that occurred prior to the required compliance date.

For each disclosure, the accounting must include the following:
The date of the disclosure;
The name of the entity or person who received the disclosure and, if known, their address;
A brief description of the PHI disclosed; and
A brief statement of the purpose of the disclosure.

Accounting for Multiple Disclosures

Multiple disclosures to the same person or entity for a single purpose may be grouped together for accounting purposes. Multiple disclosures grouped together for accounting purposes must contain the following information:
The first date during the accounting period of such disclosures;
The frequency, the elapsed time period, the number of the disclosures occurring during the accounting period; and
The date of the last such disclosure during the accounting period.

Type and Quality of The Documentation

A covered entity employer must maintain its policies and procedures in written or electronic form. If a communication is in writing, maintain it in writing, or, maintain an electronic copy, as documentation.

A written or electronic record of any required action, activity, or designation must be maintained.

A covered entity must retain the documentation for six years from the date the document was created to the date when it was last in effect, whichever is later.

Items, which must be, documented

Each and every compliance step taken.

All policies and procedures concerning HIPAA.

Any required action, activity, or designation including all decisions required by the Privacy Rule.

All complaints received and their dispositions.

Any penalties applied or disciplinary actions taken.

All disclosure accountings taken including any information required to be included in an accounting, which is provided. This includes the titles of the persons or offices responsible for receiving and processing requests for an accounting by individuals.

The certification by the plan sponsor that the plan documents have been amended to incorporate required provisions for disclosure of PHI to the sponsor.

Personnel designations.

Evidence that training has been provided.

Any signed authorization.

Compliance with the notice requirements.

The designated record sets that are subject to access by individuals and the titles of the persons or offices responsible for receiving and processing requests for access by individuals.

The titles of the persons or offices responsible for receiving and processing requests for amendments to PHI by individuals.

Designating A Privacy Officer...and A Contact Person

One of the requirements of HIPAA is to designate a Privacy Officer; and a Contact Person. The "privacy officer" is responsible for the development and implementation of the policies and procedures. The "contact person" is responsible for receiving complaints serving as the primary source of information to provide further information about matters covered by the privacy notice. It is possible for the privacy officer and the contact person to be the same person. You must document these procedures and the training you have provided.

Providing Training

Under HIPAA you must train all members of your workforce. They must have a basic understanding and knowledge of the Privacy Rule that corresponds to their job responsibilities. Also, provide training on you policies and procedures as regards privacy. Those employees with primary responsibility for compliance with the Privacy Rule need to be very well trained. (Think of the Privacy Officer or The Contact Person as examples). Those employees with limited responsibility need less training. Each situation will turn on its own merit, however, all employees who have contact with PHI, must be trained in what they can and cannot do with such information and the consequences of failing to comply with the Privacy Rule. The job descriptions of employees with access to PHI must specify their duties including their compliance responsibilities.

Training on the policies and procedures with respect to PHI must be provided no later than the compliance date for the covered entity. Each new hire must be trained within a reasonable period of time after the person joins the workforce. As changes occur in the employment situation additional training must be provided to keep the employees abreast of those changes. To protect yourself, document that the training took place.

> **Editor's Note:** Sample training programs for employees on their rights, for supervisors and managers on their responsibilities, and for Privacy Officers and Contact Persons on their duties are included on a CD-Rom provided at no additional charge to purchasers of this book.

Making It Work For You

You can fit the above requirements for various job positions and training to the needs of your organization. For example, the privacy official for the group health plan of a small employer may be the HR Manager, who will have other duties. On the other hand, the privacy official at a large health plan may be a full-time position and may have the regular support and advice of a privacy staff or board.

For smaller employers providing each employee a copy of your privacy policies and documentation requirements and taking steps to insure that each employee has reviewed the policies will, most likely, meet the training requirements. On the other hand, for supervisors, managers, and others who may have to administer the policy additional training is a good idea and it will be required.

Reducing Your Compliance Burden

Administrative Requirements:
If you are an employer with a group health plan that provides health benefits only through an insurance contract with a health insurance issuer or an HMO, and the only PHI you have is a general summary of health information or information on who is participating or is enrolled in or has withdrawn from the plan, your burden for compliance is greatly reduced and much easier to comply with.

If the health insurance issuer or HMO **only** discloses limited information to the plan sponsor, the group health plan does not have to be amended, and, it is permitted to share information with the plan sponsor. Information, which may be provided without activating the amendment requirement falls into two categories. It is sumfmary health information that the plan sponsor requests for the limited purposes of:

a)   obtaining bids for health plans costs; or

b)   modifying, amending, or terminating the group health plan.

Editor's Note: Remember, Self-insured, and/or partially self-insured group health plans are required to distribute the privacy notice.

Exception to the Privacy Notice

A group health plan that provides benefits through insurance or an HMO does not have to distribute a privacy notice. A group health plan that receives only summary health information and enrollment information has no notice requirements. This is because, generally, this notice is or will be provided by the insurer or the HMO. Regardless of the above exceptions, if you have a group health plan which provides benefits solely through insurance or an HMO **and receives more than summary health information or enrollment information you must have a privacy notice** and it must be provided upon request to employees or others enrolled in the plan.

Calculating An Acceptable Level of Risk As An Employer

The level of risk incurred in complying with HIPAA varies depending on:

1.   The amount of PHI that the plan receives, creates, and discloses;

2.   The design of the plan;

3.   The type or kind of PHI that the plan creates and receives; and

4.   The type of PHI that the plan shares with the plan sponsor.

A.   For the employer, the highest risk category of plan is the self-insured, self-administered plan that shares information beyond summary information and enrollment information with the plan sponsor. Such plans must comply with all policy and procedure requirements, adopt amendments, and implement all personnel and training provisions of the HIPAA Privacy Rule.

B.   For the employer, the next highest risk is the fully insured plans that receive more than summary information and discloses it to the plan sponsor. Generally such plans entail less risk, but, still, there must be a privacy notice available on request, it must be amended as needed, and it must adopt the full range of policies and procedures.

C.   For the employer, the next level of risk is for plans, which may or actually do, receive and/or create more than summary information but only disclose summary and enrollment information to the plan sponsor. Plans of this type have fewer compliance requirements, but they must still develop and implement all of policies and procedures and distribute a privacy notice if not fully insured.

D.   For the employer, the next level of risk is for plans, which are fully insured and receive only summary health information and/or enrollment information. Fully insured plans have the lowest compliance risk. They do not have to be amended. They do not have to have a privacy notice. They do not have to name a privacy officer. They do not have to provide training. They do not have to provide administrative, technical, and physical safeguards. They do not have to have a complaint procedure. They do not have to adopt penalties and disciplinary procedures for violations. They do not have to have a procedure to mitigate violations. And, finally, they do not have to adopt policies and procedures for Privacy Rule compliance.

E.   All of these plans, regardless of level of risk, may not intimidate, threaten, discriminate or engage in acts of retaliation because an employee has exercised his or her rights under HIPAA.

Also, the employer may not require a waiver of rights, and must comply with the documentation requirements.

Summary Of Risk Assessment

As can be seen from the above, the key for the employer to reducing risk is to limit both the plan and the employer to only summary health information and enrollment information. To reduce the burden of complying with HIPAA first look to arrange for the plan, or the employer, or both, to get by with only summary and enrollment information.

Q & A: PHI and "The Minimum Necessary Information Standard"

Q: How are covered entities expected to determine what is the minimum necessary PHI that can be used, disclosed, or requested for a particular purpose?

A: The Privacy Rule requires a covered entity to make reasonable efforts to limit use, disclosure of, and requests for PHI to the minimum necessary to accomplish the intended purpose. To allow covered entities the flexibility to address their unique circumstances, the rule requires covered entities to make their own assessment of what PHI is reasonably necessary for a particular purpose, given the characteristics of their business and workforce, and to implement policies and procedures accordingly. This is not a strict standard and covered entities need not limit information uses or disclosures to those that are absolutely needed to serve the purpose. This is a reasonableness standard that calls for an approach consistent with the best practices and guidelines already used by many providers today to limit the unnecessary sharing of medical information.

Q: Won't the minimum necessary restrictions impede the delivery of quality health care by preventing or hindering necessary exchanges of patient medical information among health care providers involved in treatment?

A: **No**. Disclosures for treatment purposes (including requests for disclosures) between health care providers are explicitly exempted from the minimum necessary requirements.

Q: **Do the minimum necessary requirements prohibit medical residents, medical students, nursing students, and other medical trainees from accessing patients' medical information in the course of their training?**

A: **No**. The definition of "health care operations" in the rule provides for "conducting training programs in which students, trainees, or practitioners in areas of health care learn under supervision to practice or improve their skills as health care providers." Covered entities can shape their policies and procedures for minimum necessary uses and disclosures to permit medical trainees access to patients' medical information, including entire medical records.

Editor's Note: For the employer the minimum standard applies both to the issue of "disclosure" and "use" of PHI. In "use" there is a requirement for the employer to identify the persons or classes of persons in its workforce who need access to "use" PHI to carry out their duties and the type or class of PHI to which they reasonable need access. In "disclosure" the minimum necessary standard requires limiting disclosure of PHI to the amount necessary to achieve the reason for the disclosure.

Q: **Must the minimum necessary standard be applied to disclosures to third parties when such disclosures are authorized by an individual?**

A: Not unless the authorization was requested by a covered entity for its own purposes. Minimum necessary does apply to authorizations requested by the covered entity for its own purposes. The Privacy Rule exempts from the minimum necessary requirements most uses or disclosures that are authorized by an individual. This includes authorizations covered entities may receive directly from third parties, such as life, disability, or casualty insurers pursuant to the patient's application for or claim under an insurance policy. For example, if a covered health care provider receives an individual's authorization to disclose medical information to a life insurer for underwriting purposes, the provider is permitted to disclose the information requested on the authorization without making any minimum necessary determination.

Q: Are providers required to make a minimum necessary determination to disclose to federal or state agencies, such as SSA or its affiliated state agencies, for individuals' applications for federal or state benefits?

A: No. Disclosures of these types **must** be authorized by an individual and, therefore, are exempt from the minimum necessary requirements. Furthermore, use of the provider's own authorization form is not required. Providers can accept an agency's authorization form. For example, disclosures to SSA (or its affiliated state agencies) for purposes of determining eligibility for disability benefits are currently made subject to an individual's completed SSA authorization form. After the compliance date, the current process may continue subject only to modest changes in the SSA authorization form to conform to the requirements.

Q: Doesn't the minimum necessary standard conflict with the Transactions standards? Does minimum necessary apply to the standard transactions?

A: No. Because the Privacy Rule exempts from the minimum necessary standard any uses or disclosures that are required for compliance with the applicable requirements of the Transactions Standard. This includes all data elements that are required or required in the standard transactions. However, in many cases, covered entities have significant discretion as to the information included in these transactions. This standard does apply to those optional data elements.

Q: In limiting access, are covered entities required to completely restructure existing workflow systems, including redesigns of office space and upgrades of computer systems, in order to comply with the minimum necessary requirements?

A: No. The basic standard for minimum necessary uses requires that covered entities make reasonable efforts to limit access to PHI to those in the workforce that need access based on their roles in the covered entity. The Department generally does not consider facility redesigns as necessary to meet the reasonableness standard for minimum necessary uses. However, covered entities may need to make certain adjustments to their facilities to minimize access, such as isolating and locking file cabinets or records rooms, or providing additional security, such as passwords, on computers maintaining personal information.

Q: Do the minimum necessary requirements prohibit covered entities from maintaining patient medical charts at bedside, require that covered entities shred empty prescription vials, or require that X-ray light boards be isolated?

A: No. The minimum necessary standards do not require that covered entities take any of these specific measures. Covered entities must, in accordance with other provisions of the Privacy Rule, take reasonable precautions to prevent inadvertent or unnecessary disclosures. For example, while the Privacy Rule does not require that X-ray boards be totally isolated from all other functions, it does require covered entities to take reasonable precautions to protect X-rays from being accessible to the public. We understand that these and similar matters are of special concern to many covered entities, and we will propose modifications to the rule to increase covered entities' confidence that these practices are not prohibited.

Q: Will doctors' and physicians' offices be allowed to continue using sign-in sheets in waiting rooms?

A: No they will not. HHS did not intend to prohibit the use of sign-in sheets, but the Privacy Rule is ambiguous about this common practice. Because of this HHS intends to propose modifications to the rule to clarify this issue.

Q: What happens when a covered entity believes that a request is seeking more than the minimum necessary PHI?

A: In such a situation, the Privacy Rule requires a covered entity to limit the disclosure to the minimum necessary. Where the rule permits covered entities to rely on the judgment of the person requesting the information, and if such reliance is reasonable despite concerns, the covered entity may make the disclosure as requested.

Part Six: Employer Guidelines For Compliance With The Privacy Rule

1.   Sit down. Think about it. Create a plan for compliance. A plan for compliance will be a useful defense should you be challenged about not complying. Do what you do well. Make and act on a plan.

2.   The key issue is access to PHI. Get control over PHI. What is PHI? Where does it come from? What happens to it once it is here? Who among my employees has reason to be in contact with or gain knowledge of PHI? Why do they need this contact or knowledge? Do I have any "business associates" who have contact with PHI about my employees? Once it gets here where is this PHI housed? How is it safeguarded? Do I really need all of this PHI? Can the amount of PHI be reduced? How much of this PHI is disclosed? Why is it disclosed? Can we reduce the amount of disclosure to the minimum necessary to make the process go forward?

3.   Taking Inventory: Deciding if it really is a health plan. Each and every health plan maintained by the employer should be inventoried, examined, and reviewed. What is the risk involved with each of these plans? Is this plan a Health plan as defined by HIPAA? (Check the definitions chapter.) Is it a stand-alone plan or is it part and parcel of another plan? What Do I tell the participants about each of these plans? How do I describe them? Do I describe them as group plans offering a number of services such as vision, dental, health or are these plans separate? Is there an advantage to me by grouping them together? Am I in a self-insured or partially self-insured plan? Do I have business associate contracts with TPA; PPO; HMO?

4.   What is the level of risk associated with each plan? Using the guidelines provided above assess the level of risk or exposure you have for each plan identified in (3) above. The guidelines provided above will help you to determine what specific steps will have to be implemented to complete this step. Once this is done ask yourself what you can do to reduce this risk? Determine what policies or procedures you can implement to reduce your risk. Will some plans need to be amended? What type and how much training will help you reduce your exposure? Consider combining or separating plans. There will be advantages and disadvantages to both approaches. Choose which is best in terms of ease of administration and HIPAA compliance.

5.   The "privacy officer" and the "contact person" and the role they play in your plan of compliance. Although highly unlikely it may turn out you are exempt from this requirement. Most likely you will have to create the job description for a "privacy officer" and you will have to assign those duties to someone. The same will be true for the "contact person." Unless you can establish that you are exempt you will be required to appoint a "privacy officer." Among other duties this person is responsible for policy development and implementation. You most likely will need a designated contact person, who is responsible for receiving complaints and providing additional information about compliance with the Privacy Rule. As part of your plan determine who will do this for you? What training they will need? Will this be their only job or will this be an additional responsibility? Can you combine the responsibilities of the "privacy officer" and the "'contact person?"

6.   Determining what policies and procedures you will use will be an important part of your plan for HIPAA compliance. Start by carefully evaluating the result of the risk assessment. From there you can determine which policies and procedures will be necessary to limit access to PHI. Remember these policies must be designed to comply with the standards, implementation specifications, or other requirements of the regulations. HHS allows you to design and implement "reasonable" plans. You do not need to alter the flow of work at your company. Base your policies and procedures on the size of your workforce, who has access to PHI, the number of health plans you offer; and the types of plans they are. Below is a list of the types of policies and procedures you may want to develop and implement..

Consider policies with accompanying procedures on:

Assure individual privacy rights. This includes limiting and controlling access to, or the amendment of, and/or accounting for, disclosures of PHI

Authorizations. Why are they needed, how are they obtained, who has to complete one, how long is it good for, procedure for revoking or altering.

Complaint Handling and Processing. What procedure will you use to respond to complaints from employees concerning accidental or intentional disclosures of PHI.

Disclosure of PHI. Under what conditions will PHI be disclosed? What is the mechanism for tracking and documenting disclosures? Will you disclose for public health reasons, law enforcement actions, or other legal proceedings?

Documentation. What is the basis for privacy decisions? Who makes these decisions? Will they need legal review prior to implementation?

Penalties. What penalties will you impose when an employee improperly discloses PHI? Will there be any sanctions such as suspension, demotion, verbal or written warning taken against the employee? How will you determine what is an appropriate and fair response?

Privacy Notice. Will you need a privacy notice. Will you distribute it to your employees? How will you inform your employees of their rights under the Privacy Rule? How will you document this?

Retaliation. Will you need a policy prohibiting retaliation against an employee or associate of an employee for exercising their rights under the Privacy Rule.

Security. How will you protect PHI? What administrative, physical or technical safeguards can you develop and implement? How will you verify the identity of a person requesting PHI? What will be your process for recognizing a "personal representative?"

Training. What training will you provide to your employees concerning their rights under the Privacy Rule? Will the training for supervisors, managers and executives be different and if yes in what way?

Waivers. Remember to include in your policies and procedures that HIPAA expressly prohibits requiring employees to sign waivers of their privacy rights.

HHS has not provided or recommended a required format for these policies. **It is strongly urged that once written these policies be submitted for legal review by a competent attorney specializing in employment law.**

7.   **Amend Plan Documents as Necessary**. Most likely you will have to adopt amendments to your plan documents. Work with your plan provider or administrator on this issue. If you are the administrator, (as in a self insured plan) seek legal assistance in this matter. Sample plan amendment is included in the Appendix.

8.   **Develop Job Descriptions**. Job descriptions are tricky. Will the role of the Privacy Officer be a separate position or will it be an additional responsibility for an existing employee? The key positions under the Privacy Rule are Privacy Officer and Contact Person. However, if in your inventory of PHI you realized that many employees in the everyday course of their duties have access to PHI, then their job descriptions should be changed to reflect that fact. Additionally you may want to consider providing these employees with training on the Privacy Rule. This training should make clear that penalties including employee disciplinary processes may result for violations of HIPAA. A sample job description is included in the Appendix.

9. Develop and Implement A Privacy Notice. An example is provided in the Appendix.

10. Develop and Implement Authorization Forms. Determine by policy when you will use Authorization forms. Remember these forms are not required for routine disclosures of PHI necessary for treatment, payment or healthcare operations (TPO: See the "Definitions Chapter for a full understanding of TPO). Also, providing PHI to the plan sponsor does not require the use of an authorization. Consider the use of a blanket authorization signed and acknowledged by all employees regarding these routine disclosures.

11. Develop and Provide Training. Just think of it this way. Any employee you have who has contact with PHI in the daily and customary performance of their job should be trained on the Privacy Rule. The training should be tailored to the level of contact they have and the exposure you have as an employer. Document the training. Repeat it annually. The training should cover adopted policies; procedures to support those policies; and address legal concerns as well as possible penalties. All employees should be provided with training and information on their rights under the Privacy Rule and the process for complaining if they believe there has been a violation of their rights.
Important: Implement a procedure to keep these complaints in house.

12. Compliance With Other Laws. There are other laws that regulate access to, use of, and disclosure of PHI. You may be covered by these laws and by the Privacy rule. Laws that may affect you as relates to PHI are: ADA; FMLA; WC; OSHA; and Drug Testing. In addition to these laws you may be currently engaged in activities on the job that will fall under the purview of the Privacy Rule because they disclose to the employer PHI. Examples of these include: Pre-employment Physicals; On site-medical clinics; EAPs; Fit for duty exams; Paid or unpaid sick leave policies; and Light duty jobs. Your plan for compliance should incorporate how you will coordinate the requirements under these various laws and/or policies into your requirements under the Privacy Rule.

The "Dos and Don'ts" of HIPAA Privacy Rule Compliance.

Do's	Don'ts
Have a plan for compliance.	Mis-use PHI.
Do document how you process PHI.	Disclose PHI unnecessarily.
Implement physical, administrative, and technical safeguards for access to PHI.	Use PHI as the basis for employment related decisions.
Separate PHI from other non-PHI information you have on employees.	Threaten employees for exercising their rights under the Privacy Rule.
Have and use authorization forms.	Use PHI for marketing programs.
Obtain "consent" to release PHI.	Fail to respond to employee complaints.
Train your employees at all levels.	Think the law does not apply to you.
Take steps to reduce amount of PHI.	
Impose punishment for non-compliance.	
Coordinate Privacy Rule with other laws.	
Make a good faith effort to comply.	
Get legal review of your compliance plan.	

Appendix

Certifications and Documents:

Example of a Plan Sponsor Certification
The plan sponsor of the group health plan certifies that it will:

1. Not use or disclose the information other than permitted by the plan document or required by law.
2. Ensure that any of its agents, including a subcontractor, to whom it provides PHI agree to the same restrictions that apply to the plan sponsor with respect to such information.
3. Not use or disclose the information for employment related actions and decisions or in connection with any other benefit or employee benefit plan of the plan sponsor.
4. Report to the group health plan any use or disclosure of the information that is inconsistent with the permitted uses or disclosures provided for of which it becomes aware.
5. Provide an individual with access to inspect or to obtain a copy of the protected health information that the plan has about the individual upon request.
6. Make available protected health information for amendment and incorporate any required amendments to protected health information.
7. Make available the information required to provide an accounting of disclosures of PHI about an individual.
8. Make its internal practices, books, and records relating to the use and disclosure of protected health information received from the group health plan available to the Secretary for purposes of determining compliance by the group health plan with this subpart.
9. If feasible, return or destroy all PHI received from the group health plan that the sponsor still maintains in any form and retain no copies of such information when no longer needed for the purpose for which disclosure was made, except that, if such return or destruction is not feasible, limit further uses and disclosures to those purposes that make the return or destruction of the information infeasible.
10. Ensure the adequate separation between the plan and the plan sponsor is established.

Michael Murphy; Mark Waterfill; Janet Braun

Sample One: General HIPAA Health Information Privacy Policy

(This sample would be good for use by an employer or plan sponsor that receives only summary health information from the plan and the insurer or HMO only performs enrollment, changes in enrollment, and payroll deductions).

Policy: It is the policy of the company to fully comply with all laws and regulations regarding and controlling the privacy or protected health information (PHI) as defined in the HIPPA Privacy Rule. The company, as plan sponsor, has adopted this policy to comply with these regulations

Definitions:

1.   PHI is defined as individuality identifiable health information received by the company's group health plan and created or received by a healthcare provider, health plan, or healthcare clearinghouse that relates to the past, present, or future health of an individual; the provision of health care to an individual; or the past, present, or future payment for the provision of health care. PHI includes health status, medical condition, claims experience, receipt of health care, medical history, genetic information, and evidence of insurability and disability.

2.   PHI does not refer to health information received apart from a group health plan, such as workers' compensation, short term disability, long term disability, medical information received based upon the Americans with Disabilities Act (ADA), medical information received based upon the Family and Medical Leave Act (FMLA), or pre-employment physicals. However, this policy on medical privacy will apply to such information.

3.   Summary health information means claims history, claims expenses, or type of claims experienced from which the following information has been deleted:

- Names
- Street address, city, county, ZIP code (except that geographic information may be aggregated by a five-digit ZIP code.
- All elements of dates (except year)
- Telephone numbers
- FAX numbers
- Electronic-mail addresses
- Social security numbers
- Medical records numbers
- Health plan beneficiary numbers
- Account numbers
- Certificate/license numbers
- Vehicle identifiers and serial numbers, including license plate numbers
- Device identifiers and serial numbers
- Web Universal Resource Locators (URL)
- Internet Protocol (IP) address numbers
- Biometric identifiers, including fingerprints and voiceprints
- Full-face photographic images and any comparable images
- Any other unique identifying number, characteristic, or code

Comment:

1.   The company sponsors a group healthcare plan that is subject to the Privacy Rule of the Health Insurance Portability and Accountability Act (HIPAA). On the basis of that law, privacy regulations now apply to certain protected health information.

2.   The company's privacy policy concerning PHI will apply to all PHI. By this policy the Privacy Officer is designated to take the appropriate actions to assure the company is complying with all federal and state laws and regulations concerning the privacy of medical information.

3.   Customarily the company limits its access to PHI because it only performs enrollment, changes in enrollment, and payroll deductions. To the extent these processes result in the company obtaining HIPAA-protected health information (PHI), it will maintain strict security and control over that information.

4.   The company will not use or disclose PHI for any reason prohibited by law or regulation.

5.   The company's health insurance provider and its insurers HMOs and/or PPOs will only disclose summary health information to the plan sponsor for the purpose of obtaining premium bids or for the purposes of modifying, amending, or terminating the Employment Retirement Income Security Act (ERISA) healthcare plan.

6.   The group plan and its insurers HMOs will not disclose PHI to the plan sponsor. As a plan sponsor, the company will request summary health information only for the purpose of obtaining premium bids or for the purposes of modifying, amending, or terminating the ERISA healthcare plan.

7.   Before assisting employees with understanding the group health plan, filing claims, or disputing claims, the company will obtain a written authorization to access that person's protected health information.

8.   The company, as plan administrator and plan sponsor, will provide plan participants with a summary plan description. A notice of the privacy practices will be provided by the HMO or health insurer.

9.   The company will discipline (up to and including discharge) employees for improper access, use or disclosure of protected health information or other confidential medical information.

10.   The company will not take any retaliatory action against any person for filing a complaint, assisting in an investigation, or otherwise opposing any act under the HIPAA privacy regulations.

11.   PHI will be secured against unauthorized access.

12.   When protected health information is used for payment of benefits and plan operations, only the minimum necessary information will be released.

Sample Privacy Notice

Notice Concerning Health Information Practices

Date of this notice: _____.

The following policy explains how information about you, particularly information relating to your health may be used and disclosed. It explains your rights in these matters. **PLEASE READ IT CAREFULLY.** Individuals who violate this policy will be subject to the company's established disciplinary process.

1.   As your employer we do not collect Private Health Information about our employees. However, from time to time such information comes into our possession for a variety of reasons. When we receive it we take the appropriate actions to safeguard your privacy.
a.   We do not put this information in your personnel file.
b.   We secure this information in a locked compartment.
c.   We limit access to that information to those persons who have a legitimate need to know this information.

2.   We have created the position of "Privacy Officer" to make sure that all private health care information is protected and your rights are fully protected. If you have any questions in this are please contact your supervisor who will in turn pass your concerns along to the Privacy Officer.

3.   Our policy is that our employees may view the Private Health Information we have in our possession at any time. The procedure is to contact your supervisor and let him or her know that you would like to view this information. Your supervisor will contact our Human Resources people and they will make arrangements for you to view this information. Ordinarily this should not take more than a few days to set up. However, please allow up to two weeks in the event there is an unforeseen problem.

4.   Because we provide our employees with group health insurance our provider collects a great deal of information about each person who participates in the plan. This might include the following information needed to provide benefits.

a.   Enrollment information, including personal information such as your address, telephone number, date of birth, and Social Security number. This could include that you are now or have been enrolled in the plan.

b.   Information received from any of your doctor, dentist or hospital needed to pay your claims.

c.   Information about your health, such as diagnosis or previous claims payment information.

d.   Any changes you may have made in the plan, like adding or dropping a dependant.

e.   History of the plan's payments of benefits.

f.   Records related to claims that were denied and then approved or records related to care or medical case management.

g.   Or other information necessary for us to provide you with health benefits.

Understanding Your Health Record/Information

5.   It is important that each of you understand this. Every time you visit a hospital, or a doctor or a dentist a record is made of that visit. Usually you give the provider permission or consent to treat you or a member of our family. In most cases these records include symptoms, results of various examinations, tests, diagnoses, treatment received, and date and time of next visit if necessary. Many times it will also include your name, social security number, address, age, place of employment and other necessary information. This information is used for a variety of purposes.

a.   To plan your care and treatment.

b.   To inform other health professionals who may treat you or provide care.

c.   To create a legal record describing the care you received.

d.   To verify that services billed were actually provided.

e.   In the event a government agency such as the board of health may want to know what you were being seen for.

f.   Or other reasons related to research, or treatment planning.

6.   You have the right to know what is in your record and how your health information is used. This right helps you in the following ways.

a.   You can make sure the information is accurate.

b.   You can get a better understanding about who else has access your health information and why.

c.   To help you make up your mind if this information should be released to others and why.

Your Rights About Your Private Health Information

7.   As strange as it may seem the record of your health care actually belongs to the group health insurance provider; or the administrator of the plan, or the doctor or dentist, or the hospital that collected it, and this information also belongs to you. Because it is your Private Health Information you have certain rights.

a.   You can request that the permitted use and disclosures of your information for treatment, payment, and healthcare operations purposes and disclosures be restricted to family members for care purposes.

b.   You can request a hard copy of this notice.

c.   You can inspect and/or obtain a copy of your health records. You have to make this request in writing and send it to the plan privacy officer.

d.   You can make changes or amend your health record. Again the request to do this must be made in writing and be submitted to the plan privacy officer. In that written request you must include a reason why you want to do this.

e.   You can request a record of who and why this information was disclosed to during the previous six years. Again the request to do this must be made in writing and be submitted to the plan privacy officer.

f.   You can request that all communication of or about your health information be delivered by alternative means or sent to alternative locations.

g.   You can revoke any authorization you have given for the use or disclosure of your private health information. However, if prior to this request the information has already been disclosed it cannot be undone.

The Responsibilities of the Group Health Plan

8.   The group healthcare plan is required to:

a.   Maintain the privacy of your health information.

b.   Provide you with a notice similar to this one explaining their legal duties and privacy practices with respect to information that is collected and maintained about you.

c.   Abide by the terms of the notice.

d.   Let you know if they are not able to abide by a restriction you a requested.

e.   Comply with any requests you may have made to have your private health information communicated by alternative means or to different al location.

f.   Restrict access to your personal health information to those individuals who need to know that information to manage the plan and its benefits.

g.   To develop and maintain physical, electronic, and procedural safeguards that comply with federal regulations concerning protecting your personal information.

9.   Under HIPAA's Privacy Rule, individuals with access to plan information has to take steps to protect that information.

a.   They must safeguard and secure the confidential personal financial information and health information as required by law.

b.   They can only use or disclose your private health information without your authorization for purposes of treatment, payment, or healthcare operations.

c. They can only disclose your private health information for administrative purposes.

d. They must limit the collection, disclosure, and use of your private healthcare information to the least amount needed to administer the plan.

e. They can allow only persons who are trained, and are authorized individuals to have access to private health information.

Working With Your Family Or A Personal Representative.

10.   The company may disclose to your family-member; your guardian, or any other person who **you** identify, your private health information needed so that person can assist you in obtaining healthcare benefits or other information needed.

11.   As part of this communication process we may use or disclose information in order to notify a family member, a personal representative, or another person who is responsible for your care, of your location, your general condition, the benefits to which you are entitled, or if you are enrolled in the group health plan.

Business associates.

12.   There are some services provided to the group health plan through outside sources. These service providers are referred to as "business associates." Accountants, attorneys, medical or financial consultants, managed care providers, claims processing service providers, claims auditors or monitors, providers of rehabilitation services would all be considered business associates.

13.   From time to time, in the course of providing these services it may be necessary to disclose your private health information to a business associate. To protect your private health information business associates are required to enter into signed agreements stating they will protect and safeguard such information including limiting access to it.

Coordination of Benefits

14.   Some employees are insured by more than one insurance company. If this is true for you it may be necessary to disclose your private health information in order to coordinate benefits. We will request prior authorization from you before this happens.

Worker's Compensation and On The Job Injuries or Illness.

15.   We may disclose your private health information necessary to comply with laws relating to workers' compensation or other similar programs established by law.

Request By Law Enforcement.

16.   We may disclose your private health information because we are required to do so by law or in response to a court order or a valid subpoena.

Selling the Company.

17.   We may disclose your private health information to the extent it is necessary if the company is being sold.

Right To Change The Privacy Restrictions

18.   We reserve the right to change our practices and/or to make the new provisions effective for all protected health information . we maintain. If this happens we will mail a revised notice to the address supplied by each employee.

19.   The group health plan will not use or disclose your private health information without your authorization unless we have told you we would in this notice.

I You Need More Information or You Want to Report a Problem

20.   If you have questions and would like additional information, you may contact _____Name Here_____

at _____ Phone Number Here .

Your Right To Complain and Non-Retaliation

21.   Internally if you believe your privacy rights have been violated, you can file a complaint with the Privacy Officer. Externally you can file a complaint with the Secretary of Health and Human Services.

22.   No action of a retaliatory nature will be taken against any employee for filing a complaint. HHS provides for severe civil and criminal penalties for violations of the Privacy Rule.

Michael Murphy; Mark Waterfill; Janet Braun

First Sample Job Description
Title: Privacy Officer

Overview: The Privacy Officer is responsible for the organization's privacy program and all associated policies and procedures.

Essential Functions: The following functions have been determined by the employer to be essential to the effective performance of this position. To the extent necessary the employer is prepared to provide reasonable accommodation to allow an applicant or incumbent to perform these essential functions, provided that person is a qualified individual with a disability as defined under the ADA.

1.   Develops and implements comprehensive, company-wide privacy programs.

2.   Takes appropriate actions to establish and maintain compliance with federal and state laws related to privacy, security, confidentiality, and protection of information including private health information, (PHI).

3.   Acts as company representative in dealings with to regulatory agencies in matters relating to privacy and security, including private health information, (PHI).

4.   Interfaces with other individuals and groups to assure policies and procedures relating to privacy, use, disclosure, and security of private health information, (PHI) are developed and implemented for organization-wide systems.

5.   Interfaces with external organizations such as legal counsel, and internal departments such as corporate compliance, human resources, accounting, information technology, or others to assure compliance with specific privacy requirements, including private health information, (PHI).

6.   Develops, implements and monitors all systems utilized for privacy compliance, including private health information, (PHI).

7.   Develops and implements required privacy policies and procedures. These include but are not limited to:

- Security of protected health information (PHI);
- Use and disclosure of PHI;
- Individual requests for restriction of use and disclosure of PHI;
- Access to, inspection of, and copying of PHI;
- Amendment and correction of PHI;
- Accounting of disclosures;
- Record keeping procedures; and
- Administrative procedures.

8.   Develops, implements, and administers company-wide procedure for requesting access to or disclosure of, protected health information.

9.   Develops and implements a procedure for verifying the legitimacy of requests for access to or disclosure of protected health information, (PHI).

10.   Interfaces with the organization's contact person in support of concerns expressed about use or disclosure or PHI.

11.   Responds appropriately to internal and/or external inquiries regarding the organization's privacy policies and procedures.

12.   Records and documents all complaints or questions concerning use or disclosure of PHI and their resolution

13.   Investigates all allegations of non-compliance with the corporate privacy policies or notice of information practices.

14.   Develops and implements training program related to privacy issues with particular emphasis on PHI. At a minimum this includes the following:

- Initial training of all employees relating to their rights, use and disclosure of PHI;
- Required retraining for all employees on their rights, use and disclosure of PHI provided at a minimum every three years; and
- Training to all employees, volunteers, trainees, and other persons under their direct or indirect control identified as likely to have access to PHI.

15.   In conjunction with the Human Resources Department develops appropriate sanctions for failure to comply with privacy policies and procedures.

16.   In conjunction with the Human Resources Department takes appropriate actions to ensure there is no intimidating, discriminatory, or other retaliatory actions taken against a person who files, testifies, assists or participates in any investigation, compliance review, proceeding or hearing related to a privacy violation or opposed any unlawful act or practice.

17.   Develops and implements mitigation procedures to be used in the event of inappropriate access to, use or disclosure of by members of PHI.

18.   As necessary revises privacy policies and procedures.

Minimum Requirements and Qualifications:

Education: A four-year degree from an accredited institution with emphasis in business administration or in a related field of study.

Experience: Minimum of five years of experience working in a professional capacity in a position of responsibility for internal organizational policy and procedures.

Knowledge Skills and Abilities: KSAs

Knowledge of HIPAA Privacy Rule.
Knowledge of security systems and methods.
Knowledge of policy development and implementation.

Ability to use computers and other electronic storage mediums.
Ability to implement administrative, technical and physical safeguards,
Ability to use computer hardware and software to develop and present training programs.
Ability to organize tasks and functions to complete work in a timely manner,
Ability to work effectively with minimum supervision.
Ability to interact effectively with others. Position requires incumbent to work effectively will employees and non-employees at all levels of the organization to explain and deal effectively with complex information and topics.
Ability to travel to off employer premises not under the direct control of the organization to perform tasks and services required in the position.

Skilled in developing and presenting training programs, and other methods for disseminating information.
Skilled in developing and implementing policies and procedures.

Places Where The Work Is Performed: This work is performed on the employer's premises. The employer's premises are fully accessible. Some functions may need to be performed in locations that are not under the control of the employer.

Equipment Used: Standard office equipment, computers, telephones, fax machines, etc.

Second Example Privacy Officer Job Description

Title: Privacy Officer

Purpose of the Position: To have available a person who is responsible for the organization's compliance with the Health Insurance Portability and Accountability Act (HIPAA) Privacy Rule. Has additional responsibility for compliance with state laws, regarding confidentiality of protected health information (PHI).

Essential Functions: The following functions have been determined by the employer to be essential to the effective performance of this position. To the extent necessary the employer is prepared to provide reasonable accommodation to allow an applicant or incumbent to perform these essential functions, provided that person is a qualified individual with a disability as defined under the ADA.

1. Conducts research to develop information needed for the development and implementation of privacy policies and procedures.
2. Identifies sources of PHI and determines who(m) has access to PHI.
3. Undertakes HIPAA risk assessment to determine level of organizational exposure to risk related to access to, use and disclosure of, PHI.
4. Acting in conjunction with others develops, implements and maintains required documents under the HIPAA Privacy Rule including amendments to plans, authorization notices, and other required materials.
5. Develops and provides required training of employees on HIPAA compliance and their rights under HIPAA.
6. Creates business associate agreements as necessary and monitors performance of business associates under those agreements to ensure compliance with HIPAA Privacy Rule requirements.
7. Creates a procedure for tracking PHI movement throughout the organization.

8. Serves as the organization's representative to determine the rights of individuals to inspect, amend, and restrict access to their PHI when requested.
9. Develops and implements policies and procedures for receiving, investigating, and resolving complaints about the plan's privacy policies and procedures. This procedure includes possible sanctions and mitigation in the event of failure to comply with privacy requirements under HIPAA.
10. Maintains a library of items related to HIPAA, the Privacy Rule, and state law where applicable, to assure current knowledge of privacy laws and regulations.
11. Serves as the company's representative in dealings external regulatory agencies such as the Department of Health and Human Services, the Office of Civil Rights or other legal entities.

Minimum Requirements and Qualifications:

Education: A four-year degree from an accredited institution with emphasis in business administration or in a related field of study.

Experience: Minimum of five years of experience working in a professional capacity in a position of responsibility for internal organizational policy and procedures.

Knowledge Skills and Abilities: KSAs

Knowledge of HIPAA Privacy Rule.
Knowledge of security systems and methods.
Knowledge of policy development and implementation.

Ability to use computers and other electronic storage mediums.
Ability to implement administrative, technical and physical safeguards,
Ability to use computer hardware and software to develop and present training programs.

Michael Murphy; Mark Waterfill; Janet Braun

Ability to organize tasks and functions to complete work in a timely manner,

Ability to work effectively with minimum supervision.

Ability to interact effectively with others. Position requires incumbent to work effectively will employees and non-employees at all levels of the organization to explain and deal effectively with complex information and topics.

Ability to travel to off employer premises not under the direct control of the organization to perform tasks and services required in the position.

Skilled in developing and presenting training programs, and other methods for disseminating information.

Skilled in developing and implementing policies and procedures.

Places Where The Work Is Performed: This work is performed on the employer's premises. The employer's premises are fully accessible. Some functions may need to be performed in locations that are not under the control of the employer.

Equipment Used: Standard office equipment, computers, telephones, fax machines, etc.

Editor's Note: Designation of a Contact Person as a provision of the Privacy Policy. The following provision could be inserted in this job description where the Privacy Officer also serves as the contact person under the HIPAA Privacy Rule.

"This position is responsible for receiving complaints of violations of the HIPAA Privacy Rule, the organization's and its group health plan's policies and procedures relating to the confidentiality of protected health information, and for providing further information about matters covered by the notice. This position requires thorough knowledge of the HIPAA Privacy Rule as well as state laws regulating access to PHI."

Suggested Policy on Training, Sanctions, & Mitigation

HIPAA Privacy Rule:
A. Training

All employees who have access to PHI as described in the HIPAA Privacy Rule are required by the company to receive training on the Privacy Rule. The intent of the training is to provide sufficient and necessary knowledge of the Privacy Rule as it relates to individual job responsibilities and of the group health plan's policies and procedures that impact on their job duties. For some positions, the access to PHI is so great that successfully completing training on the requirements of the HIPAA Privacy Rule and the company's policies and procedures regarding access to, use and disclosure of, PHI is required for the position.

B. Sanctions

The company has developed reasonable and necessary sanctions that the company will implement in the event of a breach of the Privacy Rule. The level of sanctions applied will be commensurate and appropriate to the severity of the violation. The application of a certain sanction in a given situation does not compel or require the company to use the same level of sanctions for a similar or identical violation occurring in the future. The company reserves the right to determine the appropriate level of sanctions based on the circumstances of a particular situation. Employees who violate the requirements of the HIPAA Privacy Rule may be subjected to the company's progressive discipline policy, up to and including termination.

C. Mitigation

Depending on the circumstances in a particular situation the company may undertake to "mitigate" the impact of a violation of the HIPAA Privacy Rule. The company has developed a number of mitigation devices and strategies it may use for this purpose. The application of a certain mitigation device or strategy in a given situation does not compel or require the company to use the same mitigation device or strategy for a similar or identical violation occurring in the future. The company reserves the right to determine the appropriate mitigation device or strategy based on the circumstances of a particular situation.

Sample Policy On Safeguards Administrative, Physical, and Technical Safeguards of PHI.

Policy: It is the policy of the company in conjunction with the administrator of the group health plan and designated "Business Associates" to provide administrative, physical, and technical safeguards of PHI.

Comment:

1.   The Privacy Officer will be responsible to develop and implement safeguards (physical, administrative and technical, which will be applied to limit access to, unnecessary use or disclosure of PHI.

a.   Additionally it is the responsibility of all employees, supervisors and managers to support and adhere to this policy.

b.   Suspected violations of this policy are to be reported to the Privacy Officer.

2.   Access to PHI is limited to employees whose job duties require such access. Employees whose positions do not require access to PHI will not be allowed access to protected health information.

3.   Hard copy records containing PHI will be isolated from other records and stored in locked cabinets and then housed in a locked room. Access to those records will be limited to those employees whose position demonstrates a legitimate need to know.

4.   PHI held in electronic format will be secured in a separate hard drive recording medium that will not be accessible by use of the company's customary data base management system. Access to this electronic storage device will be limited to those employees whose position demonstrates a legitimate need to know. Accessing this

information will be further protected by use of required, specifically assigned passwords and user names. a password. The Privacy Officer will maintain a log of assigned user names and passwords assigned to identified employees. The IT department will monitor "log-ons" to the restricted storage device and report violations to the Privacy Officer.

5.   By this policy no PHI will be transmitted electronically without the prior approval of the Privacy Officer, or in that person's absence by the IT department. When PHI is transmitted electronically it must be properly protected by encryption software.

a.   Additionally the company has installed a designated fax machine located in an area with limited access will be used for sending and receiving documents that include protected health information.

b.   E-mails containing protected health information will be immediately filed in a secure area of the computer network and all other copies will be deleted.

6.   Employees whose positions require them to have access to PHI, are not to discuss PHI with other employees unless there is a legitimate need to know. When necessary to discuss PHI those employees must take reasonable measures to assure these discussions are not overheard.

7.   Questions or concerns about this policy are to be directed to the Privacy Officer.

8.   Violations of this policy may result in disciplinary action against the employee up to and including termination. Beyond that regulatory agencies may file a legal action against those employees resulting in fines and possible imprisonment.

Michael Murphy; Mark Waterfill; Janet Braun

Sample Policy on Minimum and Necessary Standards

Minimum and Necessary Standards For Use and Disclosure of PHI.

Policy: It is the policy of the company in conjunction with the administrator of the group health plan and designated "Business Associates" to only use and disclose the minimum necessary protected health information (PHI) to accomplish the purpose for which that the information is being used or disclosed.

Comment:

1.   The Privacy Officer will be responsible to develop and implement the minimum necessary standards for use or disclosure of PHI.

a.   Additionally it is the responsibility of all employees, supervisors and managers to support and adhere to this policy.

b.   Suspected violations of this policy are to be reported to the Privacy Officer.

2.   The use and disclosure of PHI is limited to employees whose job duties require this activity. Employees whose positions do not require this activity will not be allowed to use or disclose protected health information.

3.   When a request is made for the use or disclosure of PHI, the company will only allow the minimum necessary PHI to be used or disclosed to accomplish the purpose of the request.

4.   The Privacy Officer will determine the minimum necessary amount of PHI to be used or disclosed. This determination will be based on the totality of the facts and circumstances in each situation. In making this determination the Privacy Officer will consider the minimum amount "reasonably" necessary to accomplish the purpose of the request.

5.   Persons making the request may appeal the decision of the privacy officer regarding the use and disclosure of PHI. The company has established a health information privacy complaint procedure for that process.

6.   Under the HIPAA Privacy Rule the following uses and disclosures of PHI are exempt from the minimum and necessary standard requirement:

- Disclosures to or requests by providers for treatment.
- Disclosures to the individual who are the subject of the information.
- Disclosures made pursuant to an individual's authorization.
- Disclosures to the U.S. Department of Health and Human Services for enforcement purposes.
- Uses or disclosures required by law.
- Use or disclosures required for compliance with HIPAA Administrative Simplification Rules

7.   Under the HIPAA Privacy Rule some disclosures are referred to as "routine" disclosures. The Privacy Officer will determine which requests for use or disclosure of PHI are routine. Once routing disclosures have been identified and classified as such employees whose position requires them to have access to PHI will be designated to make routine disclosures. The following are examples of routine disclosures.

a.   Provider requests about whether an individual is covered by the plan for purposes of filing a claim. The provider must provides the individual's membership number. This information may be disclosed by the employee responsible for this information without review by the privacy officer.

b.   Provider requests information about the status of a claim. The claims administrator may disclose that the claim has been decided or is pending without review by the privacy officer.

If the claim has been decided, the disclosure of that information and the reason for the decision may be released by the claims administrator without review by the privacy officer.

8.   Questions or concerns about this policy are to be directed to the Privacy Officer.

9.   Violations of this policy may result in disciplinary action against the employee up to and including termination. Beyond that regulatory agencies may file a legal action against those employees resulting in fines and possible imprisonment.

Sample Policy, Authorization to Disclose Protected Health Information

Policy: It is the policy of the company in conjunction with the administrator of the group health plan and designated "Business Associates" that except where permitted, the company will not request or disclose protected health information (PHI) without a valid authorization.

Comment:

1.   The Privacy Officer will be responsible to develop and implement a valid authorization form to be used to authorize use or disclosure of PHI.

a.   Additionally it is the responsibility of all employees, supervisors and managers to support and adhere to this policy.
b.   Suspected violations of this policy are to be reported to the Privacy Officer.

2.   The use and disclosure of PHI is limited to employees whose job duties require this activity. Employees whose positions do not require this activity will not allow the use or disclosure of PHI without prior approval o f the Privacy Officer.

3.   PHI must be disclosed to the individual when requested and during compliance investigations.

4.   The plan Privacy Officer will determine if an authorization request directed to the group health plan meets the requirements of the HIPAA Privacy Rule.

5.   A valid authorization must contain at least the following requirements:

- A specific and meaningful description of the information to be used or disclosed.
- The name or other specific identification of who is authorized to make the requested use or disclosure.
- The name or other specific identification of to whom the covered entity may make the disclosure.
- A description of each purpose of the requested use or disclosure. The statement "at the request of the individual" is a sufficient description of the purpose when an individual initiates the authorization.
- An expiration date or an expiration event that relates to the individual or the purpose of the use or disclosure. The statement "end of the research study", "none", or similar language is sufficient if the authorization is for a use or disclosure of PHI for research.
- Signature of the individual and date.

6.   If applicable, the authorization will provide notice of all the following (if applicable):

- The right to revoke the authorization in writing.
- The exceptions to the right to revoke and a description of how the individual may revoke the authorization; or a reference to the covered entity's privacy notice that includes this information.
- Whether treatment, payment, enrollment, or eligibility for benefits may or may not be conditioned on the authorization including the consequences of a refusal to sign the authorization when such a condition is allowed.
- The potential for PHI disclosed as requested by the authorization to be further disclosed by the recipient of the PHI and, therefore, no longer be protected by the HIPAA Privacy Rule.

7.   Signed authorizations will be retained for six years following the date of the expiration of the authorization.

8.   A signed copy of an authorization requested by the group
health plan will be provided to the individual.

9.   Under general circumstances an individual will be allowed to
revoke an authorization at any time. The request to revoke an
authorization must be provided in writing unless the authorization was
obtained as a condition of obtaining insurance coverage **and** the
insurer has the legal right to contest a claim under the policy or to
contest the policy itself.

10.   The following PHI may be disclosed without authorization:

- To the individual who is the subject of the information.
- For treatment, payment, or healthcare operations.
- Incident to a permitted or required disclosure as long
  as the minimum necessary and administrative,
  technical, and physical safeguards have been followed.
- Pursuant to an agreement with opportunity to agree or
  object for very limited information in certain limited
  circumstances.
- When required by law, for public health purposes, and
  similar purposes.
- To comply with worker's compensation and similar
  laws.

11.   Questions or concerns about this policy are to be directed to
the Privacy Officer.

12.   Violations of this policy may result in disciplinary action
against the employee up to and including termination. Beyond that
regulatory agencies may file a legal action against those employees
resulting in fines and possible imprisonment.

Michael Murphy; Mark Waterfill; Janet Braun

STANDARDS FOR PRIVACY OF INDIVIDUALLY IDENTIFIABLE HEALTH INFORMATION [*45 CFR Parts 160 and 164*]

> **Editor's Note:** The following information was developed and provided by the Department of Health and Human Services. It is provided here as an additional source of information concerning the Privacy Rule under HIPAA. The authors take no responsibility for its accuracy. Areas in **bold** were emphasized by the authors.

The following is an overview that provides answers to general questions regarding the regulation entitled, *Standards for Privacy of Individually Identifiable Health Information* (the Privacy Rule), promulgated by the Department of Health and Human Services (HHS), and process for modifications to that rule. Detailed guidance on specific requirements in the regulation is presented in subsequent sections, each of which addresses a different standard.

The Privacy Rule provides the first comprehensive federal protection for the privacy of health information. All segments of the health care industry have expressed their support for the objective of enhanced patient privacy in the health care system. At the same time, HHS and most parties agree that privacy protections must not interfere with a patient's access to or the quality of health care delivery.

The guidance provided in this section and those that follow is meant to communicate as clearly as possible the privacy policies contained in the rule. Each section has a short summary of a particular standard in the Privacy Rule, followed by Questions and Answers about that provision. In some cases, the guidance identifies areas of the Privacy Rule where a modification or change to the rule is necessary. These areas are summarized below in response to the question "What changes might you make to the final rule?" and discussed in more detail in the subsequent sections of this guidance.

We emphasize that this guidance document is only the first of several technical assistance materials that we will issue to provide clarification and help covered entities implement the rule. We anticipate that there will be many questions that will arise on an ongoing basis, which we will need to answer in future guidance. In addition, the Department will issue proposed modifications as necessary in one or more rulemakings to ensure that patients' privacy needs are appropriately met. The Department plans to work expeditiously to address these additional questions and propose modifications as necessary.

Questions and Answers About The Privacy Rule

Q: What does this regulation do?

A: The Privacy Rule became effective on April 14, 2001. Most health plans and health care providers that are covered by the new rule must comply with the new requirements by April 2003. The Privacy Rule, for the first time, creates national standards to protect individuals' medical records and other personal health information.

> It gives patients more control over their health information.
> It sets boundaries on the use and release of health records.
> It establishes appropriate safeguards that health care providers and others must achieve to protect the privacy of health information.
> It holds violators accountable, with civil and criminal penalties that can be imposed if they violate patients' privacy rights.
> And it strikes a balance when public responsibility requires disclosure of some forms of data – for example, to protect public health.

For patients – it means being able to make informed choices when seeking care and reimbursement for care based on how personal health information may be used.

It enables patients to find out how their information may be used and what disclosures of their information have been made.

It generally limits release of information to the minimum reasonably needed for the purpose of the disclosure.

It gives patients the right to examine and obtain a copy of their own health records and request corrections.

Q: Why is this regulation needed?

A: In enacting the Health Insurance Portability and Accountability Act of 1996 (HIPAA), Congress mandated the establishment of standards for the privacy of individually identifiable health information.

When it comes to personal information that moves across hospitals, doctors' offices, insurers or third party payers, and state lines, our country has relied on a patchwork of federal and state laws. Under the current patchwork of laws, personal health information can be distributed – without either notice or consent – for reasons that have nothing to do with a patient's medical treatment or health care reimbursement. Patient information held by a health plan may be passed on to a lender who may then deny the patient's application for a home mortgage or a credit card – or to an employer who may use it in personnel decisions. The Privacy Rule establishes a federal floor of safeguards to protect the confidentiality of medical information. State laws which provide stronger privacy protections will continue to apply over and above the new federal privacy standards.

Health care providers have a strong tradition of safeguarding private health information. But in today's world, the old system of paper records in locked filing cabinets is not enough. With information broadly held and transmitted electronically, the rule provides clear standards for all parties regarding protection of personal health information.

Q: What does this regulation require the average provider or health plan to do?

A: For the average health care provider or health plan, the Privacy Rule requires activities, such as:

> Providing information to patients about their privacy rights and how their information can be used.
> Adopting clear privacy procedures for its practice, hospital, or plan.
> Training employees so that they understand the privacy procedures.
> Designating an individual to be responsible for seeing that the privacy procedures are adopted and followed.
> Securing patient records containing individually identifiable health information so that they are not readily available to those who do not need them.

Responsible health care providers and businesses already take many of the kinds of steps required by the rule to protect patients' privacy. Covered entities of all types and sizes are required to comply with the final Privacy Rule. To ease the burden of complying with the new requirements, the Privacy Rule gives needed flexibility for providers and plans to create their own privacy procedures, tailored to fit their size and needs. The scalability of the rules provides a more efficient and appropriate means of safeguarding protected health information than would any single standard. For example,

The privacy official at a small physician practice may be the office manager, who will have other non-privacy related duties; the privacy official at a large health plan may be a full-time position, and may have the regular support and advice of a privacy staff or board.

The training requirement may be satisfied by a small physician practice's providing each new member of the workforce with a copy of its privacy policies and documenting that new members have reviewed the policies; whereas a large health plan may provide training through live instruction, video presentations, or interactive software programs.

The policies and procedures of small providers may be more limited under the rule than those of a large hospital or health plan, based on the volume of health information maintained and the number of interactions with those within and outside of the health care system.

Q.   Who must comply with these new privacy standards?

A: As required by Congress in HIPAA, the Privacy Rule covers health plans, health care clearinghouses, and those health care providers who conduct certain financial and administrative transactions electronically. These electronic transactions are those for which standards are required to be adopted by the Secretary under HIPAA, such as electronic billing and fund transfers. These entities (collectively called "covered entities") are bound by the new privacy standards even if they contract with others (called "business associates") to perform some of their essential functions. The law does not give HHS the authority to regulate other types of private businesses or public agencies through this regulation. For example, HHS does not have the authority to regulate employers, life insurance companies, or public agencies that deliver social security or welfare benefits. The "Business Associate" section of this guidance provides a more detailed discussion of the covered entities' responsibilities when they engage others to perform essential functions or services for them.

Q: When will covered entities have to meet these standards?

A: As Congress required in HIPAA, most covered entities have two full years from the date that the regulation took effect – or, until April 14, 2003 – to come into compliance with these standards. Under the law, small health plans will have three full years – or, until April 14, 2004 – to come into compliance. The HHS Office for Civil Rights (OCR) will provide assistance to help covered entities prepare to comply with the rule. OCR maintains a Web site with information on the new regulation, including guidance for industry, such as these frequently asked questions, at http://www.hhs.gov/ocr/hipaa/.

Q: Do you expect to make any changes to this rule before the compliance date?

A: We can and will issue proposed modifications to correct any unintended negative effects of the Privacy Rule on health care quality or on access to such care.

In February 2001, Secretary Thompson requested public comments on the final rule to help HHS assess the rule's real-world impact in health care delivery. During the 30-day comment period, we received more than 11,000 letters or comments – including some petitions with thousands of names. These comments are helping to guide the Department's efforts to clarify areas of the rule to eliminate uncertainties and to help covered entities begin their implementation efforts.

Q: What changes might you make in the final rule?

A: We continue to review the input received during the recent public comment period to determine what changes are appropriate to ensure that the rule protects patient privacy as intended without harming consumers' access to care or the quality of that care.

Examples of standards in the Privacy Rule for which we will propose changes are:

Phoned-in Prescriptions – A change will permit pharmacists to fill prescriptions phoned in by a patient's doctor before obtaining the patient's written consent (see the "Consent" section of this guidance for more discussion).

Referral Appointments – A change will permit direct treatment providers receiving a first time patient referral to schedule appointments, surgery, or other procedures before obtaining the patient's signed consent (see the "Consent" section of this guidance for more discussion).

Allowable Communications – A change will increase the confidence of covered entities that they are free to engage in whatever communications are required for quick, effective, high quality health care, including routine oral communications with family members, treatment discussions with staff involved in coordination of patient care, and using patient names to locate them in waiting areas (see the "Oral Communications" section of this guidance for more discussion).

Minimum Necessary Scope – A change will increase covered entities' confidence that certain common practices, such as use of sign-up sheets and X-ray light boards, and maintenance of patient medical charts at bedside, are not prohibited under the rule (see the "Minimum Necessary" section of this guidance for more discussion).

In addition, HHS may reevaluate the Privacy Rule to ensure that parents have appropriate access to information about the health and well being of their children. This issue is discussed further in the "Parents and Minors" section of this guidance.

Other changes to the Privacy Rule also may be considered as appropriate.

Q: How will you make any changes?

A: Any changes to the final rule must be made in accordance with the Administrative Procedures Act (APA). HHS intends to comply with the APA by publishing its rule changes in the Federal Register through a Notice of Proposed Rulemaking and will invite comment from the public. After reviewing and addressing those comments, HHS will issue a final rule to implement appropriate modifications.

Congress specifically authorized HHS to make appropriate modifications in the first year after the final rule took effect in order to ensure the rule could be properly implemented in the real world. We are working as quickly as we can to identify where modifications are needed and what corrections need to be made so as to give covered entities as much time as possible to implement the rule. Covered entities can and should begin the process of implementing the privacy standards in order to meet their compliance dates.

CONSENT [45 CFR § 164.506]

Background

The Privacy Rule establishes a federal requirement that most doctors, hospitals, or other health care providers obtain a patient's written consent before using or disclosing the patient's personal health information to carry out treatment, payment, or health care operations (TPO). Today, many health care providers, for professional or ethical reasons, routinely obtain a patient's consent for disclosure of information to insurance companies or for other purposes. The Privacy Rule builds on these practices by establishing a uniform standard for certain health care providers to obtain their patients' consent for uses and disclosures of health information about the patient to carry out TPO.

General Provisions

Patient consent is required before a covered health care provider that has a direct treatment relationship with the patient may use or disclose protected health information (PHI) for purposes of TPO. Exceptions to this standard are shown in the next bullet.

Uses and disclosures for TPO may be permitted without prior consent in an emergency, when a provider is required by law to treat the individual, or when there are substantial communication barriers.

Health care providers that have indirect treatment relationships with patients (such as laboratories that only interact with physicians and not patients), health plans, and health care clearinghouses may use and disclose PHI for purposes of TPO without obtaining a patient's

Michael Murphy; Mark Waterfill; Janet Braun

consent. The rule permits such entities to obtain consent, if they choose.

If a patient refuses to consent to the use or disclosure of their PHI to carry out TPO, the health care provider may refuse to treat the patient.

A patient's written consent need only be obtained by a provider one time.

The consent document may be brief and may be written in general terms. It must be written in plain language, inform the individual that information may be used and disclosed for TPO, state the patient's rights to review the provider's privacy notice, to request restrictions and to revoke consent, and be dated and signed by the individual (or his or her representative).

Individual Rights Concerning Consent

An individual may revoke consent in writing, except to the extent that the covered entity has taken action in reliance on the consent.

An individual may request restrictions on uses or disclosures of health information for TPO. The covered entity need not agree to the restriction requested, but is bound by any restriction to which it agrees.

An individual must be given a notice of the covered entity's privacy practices and may review that notice prior to signing a consent.

Administrative Issues Concerning Consent

A covered entity must retain the signed consent for 6 years from the date it was last in effect. The Privacy Rule does not dictate the form in which these consents are to be retained by the covered entity.

Certain integrated covered entities may obtain one joint consent for multiple entities.

If a covered entity obtains consent and also receives an authorization to disclose PHI for TPO, the covered entity may disclose information only in accordance with the more restrictive document, unless the covered entity resolves the conflict with the individual.

Transition provisions allow providers to rely on consents received prior to April 14, 2003 (the compliance date of the Privacy Rule for most covered entities), for uses and disclosures of health information obtained prior to that date.

Questions and Answers About Consent

Q.   Are health plans or clearinghouses required to obtain an individual's consent to use or disclose PHI to carry out TPO?

A: No. Health plans and clearinghouses may use and disclose PHI for these purposes without obtaining consent. These entities are permitted to obtain consent. If they choose to seek individual consent for these uses and disclosures, the consent must meet the standards, requirements, and implementation specifications for consents set forth under the rule.

Q: Can a pharmacist use PHI to fill a prescription that was telephoned in by a patient's physician if the patient is a new patient to the pharmacy and has not yet provided written consent to the pharmacy?

A: The Privacy Rule, as written, does not permit this activity without prior patient consent. It poses a problem for first-time users of a particular pharmacy or pharmacy chain. The Department of Health and Human Services did not intend the rule to interfere with a pharmacist's normal activities in this way. The Secretary is aware of this problem, and will propose modifications to fix it to ensure ready patient access to high quality health care.

Q: Can direct treatment providers, such as a specialist or hospital, to whom a patient is referred for the first time, use PHI

to set up appointments or schedule surgery or other procedures before obtaining the patient's written consent?

A: As in the pharmacist example above, the Privacy Rule, as written, does not permit uses of PHI prior to obtaining the patient's written consent for TPO. This unintended problem potentially exists in any circumstance when a patient's first contact with a direct treatment provider is not in person. As noted above, the Secretary is aware of this problem and will propose modifications to fix it.

Q: Will the consent requirement restrict the ability of providers to consult with other providers about a patient's condition?

A: No. A provider with a direct treatment relationship with a patient would have to have initially obtained consent to use that patient's health information for treatment purposes. Consulting with another health care provider about the patient's case falls within the definition of "treatment" and, therefore, is permissible. If the provider being consulted does not otherwise have a direct treatment relationship with the patient, that provider does not need to obtain the patient's consent to engage in the consultation.

Q: Does a pharmacist have to obtain a consent under the Privacy Rule in order to provide advice about over-the-counter medicines to customers?

A: No. A pharmacist may provide advice about over-the-counter medicines without obtaining the customers' prior consent, provided that the pharmacist does not create or keep a record of any PHI. In this case, the only interaction or disclosure of information is a conversation between the pharmacist and the customer. The pharmacist may disclose PHI about the customer to the customer without obtaining his or her consent (§ 164.502(a)(1)(i)), but may not otherwise use or disclose that information.

Q: Can a patient have a friend or family member pick up a prescription for her?

A: Yes. A pharmacist may use professional judgment and experience with common practice to make reasonable inferences of the patient's best interest in allowing a person, other than the patient, to pick up a prescription (see § 164.510(b)). For example, the fact that a relative or friend arrives at a pharmacy and asks to pick up a specific prescription for an individual effectively verifies that he or she is involved in the individual's care, and the rule allows the pharmacist to give the filled prescription to the relative or friend. The individual does not need to provide the pharmacist with the names of such persons in advance.

Q: The rule provides an exception to the prior consent requirement for "emergency treatment situations." How will a provider know when the situation is an "emergency treatment situation" and, therefore, is exempt from the Privacy Rule's prior consent requirement?

A: Health care providers must exercise their professional judgment to determine whether obtaining a consent would interfere with the timely delivery of necessary health care. If, based on professional judgment, a provider reasonably believes at the time the patient presents for treatment that a delay involved in obtaining the patient's consent to use or disclose information would compromise the patient's care, the provider may use or disclose PHI that was obtained during the emergency treatment, without prior consent, to carry out TPO. The provider must attempt to obtain consent as soon as reasonably practicable after the provision of treatment. If the provider is able to obtain the patient's consent to use or disclose information before providing care, without compromising the patient's care, we require the provider to do so.

Q: Does the exception to the consent requirement regarding substantial barriers to communication with the individual affect

requirements under Title VI of the Civil Rights Act of 1964 or the Americans with Disabilities Act?

A: No. The provision of the Privacy Rule regarding substantial barriers to communication does not affect covered entities' obligations under Title VI or the Americans with Disabilities Act. Entities that are covered by these statutes must continue to meet the requirements of the statutes. The Privacy Rule works in conjunction with these laws to remove impediments to access to necessary health care for all individuals.

Q: What is the difference between "consent" and "authorization" under the Privacy Rule?

A: A consent is a general document that gives health care providers, which have a direct treatment relationship with a patient, permission to use and disclose all PHI for TPO. It gives permission only to that provider, not to any other person. Health care providers may condition the provision of treatment on the individual providing this consent. One consent may cover all uses and disclosures for TPO by that provider, indefinitely. A consent need not specify the particular information to be used or disclosed, nor the recipients of disclosed information.

Only doctors or other health care providers with a direct treatment relationship with a patient are required to obtain consent. Generally, a "direct treatment provider" is one that treats a patient directly, rather than based on the orders of another provider, and/or provides health care services or test results directly to patients. Other health care providers, health plans, and health care clearinghouses may use or disclose information for TPO without consent, or may choose to obtain a consent.

An authorization is a more customized document that gives covered entities permission to use specified PHI for specified purposes, which are generally other than TPO, or to disclose PHI to a third party specified by the individual. Covered entities may not condition treatment or coverage on the individual providing an authorization. An authorization is more detailed and specific than a consent. It covers only the uses and disclosures and only the PHI stipulated in the authorization; it has an expiration date; and, in some cases, it also states the purpose for which the information may be used or disclosed.

An authorization is required for use and disclosure of PHI not otherwise allowed by the rule. In general, this means an authorization is required for purposes that are not part of TPO and not described in § 164.510 (uses and disclosures that require an opportunity for the individual to agree or to object) or § 164.512 (uses and disclosures for which consent, authorization, or an opportunity to agree or to object is not required). Situations in which an authorization is required for TPO purposes are identified and discussed in the next question.

All covered entities, not just direct treatment providers, must obtain an authorization to use or disclose PHI for these purposes. For example, a covered entity would need an authorization from individuals to sell a patient mailing list, to disclose information to an employer for employment decisions, or to disclose information for eligibility for life insurance. A covered entity will never need to obtain both an individual's consent and authorization for a single use or disclosure. However, a provider may have to obtain consent and authorization from the same patient for different uses or disclosures. For example, an obstetrician may, under the consent obtained from the patient, send an appointment reminder to the patient, but would need authorization from the patient to send her name and address to a company marketing a diaper service.

Q: Would a covered entity ever need an authorization rather than a consent for uses or disclosures of PHI for TPO?

A: Yes.   The Privacy Rule requires providers to obtain authorization and not consent to use or disclose PHI maintained in psychotherapy notes for treatment by persons other than the originator of the notes, for payment, or for health care operations purposes, except as specified in the Privacy Rule (§ 164.508(a)(2)). In addition, because the consent is only for a use or disclosure of PHI for the TPO purposes of the covered entity obtaining the consent, an authorization is also required if the disclosure is for the TPO purposes of an entity other than the provider who obtained the consent. For example, a health plan seeking payment for a particular service from a second health plan, such as in coordination of benefits or secondary payer situations, may need PHI from a physician who rendered the health care services. In this case, the provider typically has been paid, and the transaction is between the plans. Since the provider's disclosure is for the TPO purposes of the plan, it would not be covered by the provider's consent. Rather, an authorization, and not a consent, would be the proper document for the plan to use when requesting such a disclosure.

Q: Will health care providers be required to determine whether another covered entity has a more restrictive consent form before disclosing information to that entity for TPO purposes?

A: No. Generally, a consent permits only the covered entity that obtains the consent to use or disclose PHI for its own TPO purposes. Under the Privacy Rule, one covered entity is not bound by a consent or any restrictions on that consent agreed to by another covered entity, with one exception. A covered entity would be bound by the consent of another covered entity if the entities use a "joint consent," as permitted by the Privacy Rule (§ 164.506(f)).

In addition, it is possible for several entities to choose to be treated as a single covered entity under the rule, as "affiliated entities." Because affiliated entities are considered to be one covered entity under the rule, there would be only one consent and each entity would be bound by that consent (§ 164.504(d)).

Q: **What is the interaction between "consent" and "notice"?**

A: The consent and the notice of privacy practices are two distinct documents. A consent document is brief (may be less than one page). It must refer to the notice and must inform the individual that he has the opportunity to review the notice prior to signing the consent. The Privacy Rule does not require that the individual read the notice or that the covered entity explain each item in the notice before the individual provides consent. We expect that some patients will simply sign the consent while others will read the notice carefully and discuss some of the practices with the covered entity.

Q: **May consent for use or disclosure of PHI be provided electronically?**

A: Yes. The covered entity may choose to obtain and store consents in paper or electronic form, provided that the consent meets all of the requirements under the Privacy Rule, including that it be signed by the individual. Paper is not required.

Q: **Must a covered entity verify a signature on a consent form if the individual is not present when he signs it?**

A: No.

Q: **May consent be obtained by a health care provider only one time if there is a single connected course of treatment involving multiple visits?**

A: Yes. A health care provider needs to obtain consent from a patient for use or disclosure of PHI only one time. This is true regardless of whether there is a connected course of treatment or treatment for unrelated conditions. A provider will need to obtain a new consent from a patient only if the patient has revoked the consent between treatments.

Q: **If an individual consents to the use or disclosure of PHI for TPO purposes, obtains a health care service, and then revokes consent before the provider bills for such service, is the provider precluded from billing for such service?**

A: No. A health care provider that provides a health care service to an individual after obtaining consent from the individual, may bill for such service even if the individual immediately revokes consent after the service has been provided. The Privacy Rule requires that an individual be permitted to revoke consent, but provides that the revocation is not effective to the extent that the health care provider has acted in reliance on the consent. Where the provider has obtained a consent and provided a health care service pursuant to that consent with the expectation that he or she could bill for the service, the health care provider has acted in reliance on the consent. The revocation would not interfere with the billing or reimbursement for that care.

Q: **If covered providers that are affiliated or part of an organized health care arrangement are located in different states with different laws regarding uses and disclosures of health information (e.g., a chain of pharmacies), do they need to obtain a consent in each state that the patient obtains treatment?**

A: No. The consent is general and only needs to be obtained by a covered entity (or by affiliated entities or entities that are part of an organized health care arrangement) one time. The Privacy Rule does not require that the consent include any details about state law, and therefore, does not require different consent forms in each state. State law may impose additional requirements for consent forms on covered entities.

Q: **Must a revocation of consent be in writing?**

A: Yes.

Q: The Privacy Rule permits a covered entity to continue to use or disclose health information, which it has on the compliance date pursuant to express legal permission obtained from an individual prior to the compliance date. Is a form, signed by a patient prior to the compliance date of the rule that permits a provider to use or disclose information for the limited purpose of payment sufficient to meet these transition provision requirements?

A: Yes. A provider that obtains permission from a patient prior to the compliance date to use or disclose information for payment purposes may use the PHI about that patient collected pursuant to that permission for purposes of TPO. Under the transition provisions, if prior to the compliance date, a provider obtained a consent for the use or disclosure of health information for any one of the TPO purposes, the provider may use the health information collected pursuant to that consent for all three purposes after the compliance date (§ 164.532(b)). Thus, a provider that obtained consent for use or disclosure for billing purposes would be able to draw on the data obtained prior to the compliance date and covered by the consent form for all TPO activities to the extent not expressly excluded by the terms of the consent.

Q: Are health plans and health care clearinghouses required by the Privacy Rule to have some form of express legal permission to use and disclose health information obtained prior to the compliance date for TPO purposes?

A: No. Health plans and health care clearinghouses are not required to have express legal permission from individuals to use or disclose health information obtained prior to the compliance date for their own TPO purposes.

MINIMUM NECESSARY [45 CFR §§ 164.502(b), 164.514(d)]

General Requirement

The Privacy Rule generally requires covered entities to take reasonable steps to limit the use or disclosure of, and requests for protected health information (PHI) to the minimum necessary to accomplish the intended purpose. The minimum necessary provisions do not apply to the following:

> Disclosures to or requests by a health care provider for treatment purposes.
> Disclosures to the individual who is the subject of the information.
> Uses or disclosures made pursuant to an authorization requested by the individual.
> Uses or disclosures required for compliance with the standardized Health Insurance Portability and Accountability Act (HIPAA) transactions.
> Disclosures to the Department of Health and Human Services (HHS) when disclosure of information is required under the rule for enforcement purposes.
> Uses or disclosures that are required by other law.

The implementation specifications for this provision require a covered entity to develop and implement policies and procedures appropriate for its own organization, reflecting the entity's business practices and workforce. We understand this guidance will not answer all questions pertaining to the minimum necessary standard, especially as applied to specific industry practices. As more questions arise with regard to application of the minimum necessary standard to particular circumstances, we will provide more detailed guidance and clarification on this issue.

Uses and Disclosures of, and Requests for PHI

For uses of PHI, the policies and procedures must identify the persons or classes of persons within the covered entity who need access to the information to carry out their job duties, the categories or types of PHI needed, and conditions appropriate to such access. For example, hospitals may implement policies that permit doctors, nurses, or others involved in treatment to have access to the entire medical record, as needed. Case-by-case review of each use is not required. Where the entire medical record is necessary, the covered entity's policies and procedures must state so explicitly and include a justification.

For routine or recurring requests and disclosures, the policies and procedures may be standard protocols and must limit PHI disclosed or requested to that which is the minimum necessary for that particular type of disclosure or request. Individual review of each disclosure or request is not required.

For non-routine disclosures, covered entities must develop reasonable criteria for determining, and limiting disclosure to, only the minimum amount of PHI necessary to accomplish the purpose of a non-routine disclosure. Non-routine disclosures must be reviewed on an individual basis in accordance with these criteria. When making non-routine requests for PHI, the covered entity must review each request so as to ask for only that information reasonably necessary for the purpose of the request.

Reasonable Reliance

In certain circumstances, the Privacy Rule permits a covered entity to rely on the judgment of the party requesting the disclosure as to the minimum amount of information that is needed. Such reliance must be reasonable under the particular circumstances of the request. This reliance is permitted when the request is made by:

A public official or agency for a disclosure permitted under § 164.512 of the rule.

Another covered entity.

A professional who is a workforce member or business associate of the covered entity holding the information.

A researcher with appropriate documentation from an Institutional Review Board (IRB) or Privacy Board.

The rule does not require such reliance, however, and the covered entity always retains discretion to make its own minimum necessary determination for disclosures to which the standard applies.

Treatment Settings

We understand that medical information must be conveyed freely and quickly in treatment settings, and thus understand the heightened concern that covered entities have about how the minimum necessary standard applies in such settings. Therefore, we are taking the following steps to clarify the application of the minimum necessary standard in treatment settings. First, we clarify some of the issues here, including the application of minimum necessary to specific practices, so that covered entities may begin implementation of the Privacy Rule. Second, we will propose corresponding changes to the regulation text, to increase the confidence of covered entities that they are free to engage in whatever communications are required for quick, effective, high quality health care. We understand that issues of this importance need to be addressed directly and clearly to eliminate any ambiguities.

Questions and Answers About Minimum Standards

Q: How are covered entities expected to determine what is the minimum necessary information that can be used, disclosed, or requested for a particular purpose?

A: The Privacy Rule requires a covered entity to make reasonable efforts to limit use, disclosure of, and requests for PHI to the minimum necessary to accomplish the intended purpose. To allow covered entities the flexibility to address their unique circumstances, the rule requires covered entities to make their own assessment of what PHI is reasonably necessary for a particular purpose, given the characteristics of their business and workforce, and to implement policies and procedures accordingly. This is not a strict standard and covered entities need not limit information uses or disclosures to those that are absolutely needed to serve the purpose. Rather, this is a reasonableness standard that calls for an approach consistent with the best practices and guidelines already used by many providers today to limit the unnecessary sharing of medical information.

The minimum necessary standard is intended to make covered entities evaluate their practices and enhance protections as needed to prevent unnecessary or inappropriate access to PHI. It is intended to reflect and be consistent with, not override, professional judgment and standards. Therefore, we expect that covered entities will utilize the input of prudent professionals involved in health care activities when developing policies and procedures that appropriately will limit access to personal health information without sacrificing the quality of health care.

Q: Won't the minimum necessary restrictions impede the delivery of quality health care by preventing or hindering necessary exchanges of patient medical information among health care providers involved in treatment?

A: No. Disclosures for treatment purposes (including requests for disclosures) between health care providers are explicitly exempted from the minimum necessary requirements. The Privacy Rule provides the covered entity with substantial discretion as to how to implement the minimum necessary standard, and appropriately and reasonably limit access to the use of identifiable health information within the covered entity. The rule recognizes that the covered entity is in the best position to know and determine who in its workforce needs access to personal health information to perform their jobs. Therefore, the covered entity can develop role-based access policies that allow its health care providers and other employees, as appropriate, access to patient information, including entire medical records, for treatment purposes.

Q: Do the minimum necessary requirements prohibit medical residents, medical students, nursing students, and other medical trainees from accessing patients' medical information in the course of their training?

A: No. The definition of "health care operations" in the rule provides for "conducting training programs in which students, trainees, or practitioners in areas of health care learn under supervision to practice or improve their skills as health care providers." Covered entities can shape their policies and procedures for minimum necessary uses and disclosures to permit medical trainees access to patients' medical information, including entire medical records.

Q: Must minimum necessary be applied to disclosures to third parties that are authorized by an individual?

A: No, unless the authorization was requested by a covered entity for its own purposes. The Privacy Rule exempts from the minimum necessary requirements most uses or disclosures that are authorized by an individual. This includes authorizations covered entities may receive directly from third parties, such as life, disability, or casualty insurers pursuant to the patient's application for or claim under an insurance policy. For example, if a covered health care provider receives an individual's authorization to disclose medical information to a life insurer for underwriting purposes, the provider is permitted to disclose the information requested on the authorization without making any minimum necessary determination. The authorization must meet the requirements of § 164.508. However, minimum necessary does apply to authorizations requested by the covered entity for its own purposes (see § 164.508(d), (e), and (f)).

Q: Are providers required to make a minimum necessary determination to disclose to federal or state agencies, such as the Social Security Administration (SSA) or its affiliated state agencies, for individuals' applications for federal or state benefits?

A: No. These disclosures must be authorized by an individual and, therefore, are exempt from the minimum necessary requirements. Further, use of the provider's own authorization form is not required. Providers can accept an agency's authorization form as long as it meets the requirements of § 164.508 of the rule. For example, disclosures to SSA (or its affiliated state agencies) for purposes of determining eligibility for disability benefits are currently made subject to an individual's completed SSA authorization form. After the compliance date, the current process may continue subject only to modest changes in the SSA authorization form to conform to the requirements in § 164.508.

Q: Doesn't the minimum necessary standard conflict with the Transactions standards? Does minimum necessary apply to the standard transactions?

A: No, because the Privacy Rule exempts from the minimum necessary standard any uses or disclosures that are required for compliance with the applicable requirements of the subchapter. This includes all data elements that are required or situationally required in the standard transactions. However, in many cases, covered entities have significant discretion as to the information included in these transactions. This standard does apply to those optional data elements.

Q: Does the rule strictly prohibit use, disclosure, or requests of an entire medical record? Does the rule prevent use, disclosure, or requests of entire medical records without case-by-case justification?

A: No. The Privacy Rule does not prohibit use, disclosure, or requests of an entire medical record. A covered entity may use, disclose, or request an entire medical record, without a case-by-case justification, if the covered entity has documented in its policies and procedures that the entire medical record is the amount reasonably necessary for certain identified purposes. For uses, the policies and procedures would identify those persons or classes of person in the workforce that need to see the entire medical record and the conditions, if any, that are appropriate for such access. Policies and procedures for routine disclosures and requests and the criteria used for non-routine disclosures would identify the circumstances under which disclosing or requesting the entire medical record is reasonably necessary for particular purposes. In making non-routine requests, the covered entity may also establish and utilize criteria to assist in determining when to request the entire medical record.

The Privacy Rule does not require that a justification be provided with respect to each distinct medical record.

Finally, no justification is needed in those instances where the minimum necessary standard does not apply, such as disclosures to or requests by a health care provider for treatment or disclosures to the individual.

Q: In limiting access, are covered entities required to completely restructure existing workflow systems, including redesigns of office space and upgrades of computer systems, in order to comply with the minimum necessary requirements?

A: No. The basic standard for minimum necessary uses requires that covered entities make reasonable efforts to limit access to PHI to those in the workforce that need access based on their roles in the covered entity.

The Department generally does not consider facility redesigns as necessary to meet the reasonableness standard for minimum necessary uses. However, covered entities may need to make certain adjustments to their facilities to minimize access, such as isolating and locking file cabinets or records rooms, or providing additional security, such as passwords, on computers maintaining personal information.

Covered entities should also take into account their ability to configure their record systems to allow access to only certain fields, and the practicality of organizing systems to allow this capacity. For example, it may not be reasonable for a small, solo practitioner who has largely a paper-based records system to limit access of employees with certain functions to only limited fields in a patient record, while other employees have access to the complete record. Alternatively, a hospital with an electronic patient record system may reasonably implement such controls, and therefore, may choose to limit access in this manner to comply with the rule.

Q: Do the minimum necessary requirements prohibit covered entities from maintaining patient medical charts at bedside, require that covered entities shred empty prescription vials, or require that X-ray light boards be isolated?

A: No. The minimum necessary standards do not require that covered entities take any of these specific measures. Covered entities must, in accordance with other provisions of the Privacy Rule, take reasonable precautions to prevent inadvertent or unnecessary disclosures. For example, while the Privacy Rule does not require that X-ray boards be totally isolated from all other functions, it does require covered entities to take reasonable precautions to protect X-rays from being accessible to the public. We understand that these and similar matters are of special concern to many covered entities, and we will propose modifications to the rule to increase covered entities' confidence that these practices are not prohibited.

Q: Will doctors' and physicians' offices be allowed to continue using sign-in sheets in waiting rooms?

A: We did not intend to prohibit the use of sign-in sheets, but understand that the Privacy Rule is ambiguous about this common practice. We, therefore, intend to propose modifications to the rule to clarify that this and similar practices are permissible.

Q: What happens when a covered entity believes that a request is seeking more than the minimum necessary PHI?

A: In such a situation, the Privacy Rule requires a covered entity to limit the disclosure to the minimum necessary as determined by the disclosing entity. Where the rule permits covered entities to rely on the judgment of the person requesting the information, and if such reliance is reasonable despite the covered entity's concerns, the covered entity may make the disclosure as requested. Nothing in the Privacy Rule prevents a covered entity from discussing its concerns with the person making the request, and negotiating an information exchange that meets the needs of both parties. Such discussions occur today and may continue after the compliance date of the Privacy Rule.

ORAL COMMUNICATIONS [45 CFR §§ 160.103, 164.501]

Background
The Privacy Rule applies to individually identifiable health information in all forms, electronic, written, oral, and any other. Coverage of oral (spoken) information ensures that information retains protections when discussed or read aloud from a computer screen or a written document. If oral communications were not covered, any health information could be disclosed to any person, so long as the disclosure was spoken.

Providers and health plans understand the sensitivity of oral information. For example, many hospitals already have confidentiality policies and concrete procedures for addressing privacy, such as posting signs in elevators that remind employees to protect patient confidentiality.

We also understand that oral communications must occur freely and quickly in treatment settings, and thus understand the heightened concern that covered entities have about how the rule applies. Therefore, we are taking a two-step approach to clarifying the regulation with respect to these communications. First, we provide some clarification of these issues here, so that covered entities may begin implementing the rule by the compliance date. Second, we will propose appropriate changes to the regulation text to clarify the regulatory basis for the policies discussed below in order to minimize confusion and to increase the confidence of covered entities that they are free to engage in communications as required for quick, effective, and high quality health care. We understand that issues of this importance need to be addressed directly and clearly in the Privacy Rule and that any ambiguities need to be eliminated.

General Requirements

Covered entities must reasonably safeguard protected health information (PHI) – including oral information – from any intentional or unintentional use or disclosure that is in violation of the rule (see § 164.530(c)(2)). They must have in place appropriate administrative, technical, and physical safeguards to protect the privacy of PHI. "Reasonably safeguard" means that covered entities must make reasonable efforts to prevent uses and disclosures not permitted by the rule. However, we do not expect reasonable safeguards to guarantee the privacy of PHI from any and all potential risks. In determining whether a covered entity has provided reasonable safeguards, the Department will take into account all the circumstances, including the potential effects on patient care and the financial and administrative burden of any safeguards.

Covered entities must have policies and procedures that reasonably limit access to and use of PHI to the minimum necessary given the job responsibilities of the workforce and the nature of their business (see §§ 164.502(b), 164.514(d)). The minimum necessary standard does not apply to disclosures, including oral disclosures, among providers for treatment purposes. For a more complete discussion of the

Michael Murphy; Mark Waterfill; Janet Braun

minimum necessary requirements, see the fact sheet and frequently asked questions titled "Minimum Necessary."

Many health care providers already make it a practice to ensure reasonable safeguards for oral information – for instance, by speaking quietly when discussing a patient's condition with family members in a waiting room or other public area, and by avoiding using patients' names in public hallways and elevators. Protection of patient confidentiality is an important practice for many health care and health information management professionals; covered entities can build upon those codes of conduct to develop the reasonable safeguards required by the Privacy Rule.

Questions and Answers About Oral Communications

Q: If health care providers engage in confidential conversations with other providers or with patients, have they violated the rule if there is a possibility that they could be overheard?

A: The Privacy Rule is not intended to prohibit providers from talking to each other and to their patients. Provisions of this rule requiring covered entities to implement reasonable safeguards that reflect their particular circumstances and exempting treatment disclosures from certain requirements are intended to ensure that providers' primary consideration is the appropriate treatment of their patients. We also understand that overheard communications are unavoidable. For example, in a busy emergency room, it may be necessary for providers to speak loudly in order to ensure appropriate treatment. The Privacy Rule is not intended to prevent this appropriate behavior. We would consider the following practices to be permissible, if reasonable precautions are taken to minimize the chance of inadvertent disclosures to others who may be nearby (such as using lowered voices, talking apart):

Health care staff may orally coordinate services at hospital nursing stations.

Nurses or other health care professionals may discuss a patient's condition over the phone with the patient, a provider, or a family member.

A health care professional may discuss lab test results with a patient or other provider in a joint treatment area.

Health care professionals may discuss a patient's condition during training rounds in an academic or training institution.

We will propose regulatory language to reinforce and clarify that these and similar oral communications (such as calling out patient names in a waiting room) are permissible.

Q: Does the Privacy Rule require hospitals and doctors' offices to be retrofitted, to provide private rooms, and soundproof walls to avoid any possibility that a conversation is overheard?

A: No, the Privacy Rule does not require these types of structural changes be made to facilities.

Covered entities must have in place appropriate administrative, technical, and physical safeguards to protect the privacy of PHI. "Reasonable safeguards" mean that covered entities must make reasonable efforts to prevent uses and disclosures not permitted by the rule. The Department does not consider facility restructuring to be a requirement under this standard. In determining what is reasonable, the Department will take into account the concerns of covered entities regarding potential effects on patient care and financial burden.

For example, the Privacy Rule does not require the following types of structural or systems changes:

Private rooms.

Soundproofing of rooms.

Encryption of wireless or other emergency medical radio communications which can be intercepted by scanners.

Encryption of telephone systems.

Covered entities must provide reasonable safeguards to avoid prohibited disclosures. The rule does not require that all risk be eliminated to satisfy this standard. Covered entities must review their own practices and determine what steps are reasonable to safeguard their patient information.

Examples of the types of adjustments or modifications to facilities or systems that may constitute reasonable safeguards are:

Pharmacies could ask waiting customers to stand a few feet back from a counter used for patient counseling.

Providers could add curtains or screens to areas where oral communications often occur between doctors and patients or among professionals treating the patient.

In an area where multiple patient-staff communications routinely occur, use of cubicles, dividers, shields, or similar barriers may constitute a reasonable safeguard. For example, a large clinic intake area may reasonably use cubicles or shield-type dividers, rather than separate rooms.

In assessing what is "reasonable," covered entities may consider the viewpoint of prudent professionals.

Q: Do covered entities need to provide patients access to oral information?

A: No. The Privacy Rule requires covered entities to provide individuals with access to PHI about themselves that is contained in their "designated record sets." The term "record" in the term "designated record set" does not include oral information; rather, it connotes information that has been recorded in some manner.

The rule does not require covered entities to tape or digitally record oral communications, nor retain digitally or tape recorded information after transcription. But if such records are maintained and used to make decisions about the individual, they may meet the definition of "designated record set." For example, a health plan is not required to provide a member access to tapes of a telephone "advice line" interaction if the tape is only maintained for customer service review and not to make decisions about the member.

Q: Do covered entities have to document all oral communications?

A: No. The Privacy Rule does not require covered entities to document any information, including oral information, that is used or disclosed for treatment, payment or health care operations (TPO).

The rule includes, however, documentation requirements for some information disclosures for other purposes. For example, some disclosures must be documented in order to meet the standard for providing a disclosure history to an individual upon request. Where a documentation requirement exists in the rule, it applies to all relevant communications, whether in oral or some other form. For example, if a covered physician discloses information about a case of tuberculosis to a public health authority as permitted by the rule in § 164.512, then he or she must maintain a record of that disclosure regardless of whether the disclosure was made orally by phone or in writing.

Q: Did the Department change its position from the proposed rule by covering oral communications in the final Privacy Rule?

A: No. The proposed rule would have covered information in any form or medium, as long as it had at some point been maintained or transmitted electronically. Once information had been electronic, it would have continued to be covered as long as it was held by a covered entity, whether in electronic, written, or oral form.

The final Privacy Rule eliminates this nexus to electronic information. All individually identifiable health information of the covered entity is covered by the rule.

BUSINESS ASSOCIATES [45 CFR §§ 160.103, 164.502(e), 164.514(e)]

Background

By law, the Privacy Rule applies only to health plans, health care clearinghouses, and certain health care providers. In today's health care system, however, most health care providers and health plans do not carry out all of their health care activities and functions by themselves; they require assistance from a variety of contractors and other businesses. In allowing providers and plans to give protected health information (PHI) to these "business associates," the Privacy Rule conditions such disclosures on the provider or plan obtaining, typically by contract, satisfactory assurances that the business associate will use the information only for the purposes for which they were engaged by the covered entity, will safeguard the information from misuse, and will help the covered entity comply with the covered entity's duties to provide individuals with access to health information about them and a history of certain disclosures (e.g., if the business associate maintains the only copy of information, it must promise to cooperate with the covered entity to provide individuals access to information upon request). PHI may be disclosed to a business associate only to help the providers and plans carry out their health care functions – not for independent use by the business associate.

What is a "business associate"?

A business associate is a person or entity who provides certain functions, activities, or services for or to a covered entity, involving the use and/or disclosure of PHI.

A business associate is not a member of the health care provider, health plan, or other covered entity's workforce.

A health care provider, health plan, or other covered entity can also be a business associate to another covered entity.

The rule includes exceptions. The business associate requirements do not apply to covered entities who disclose PHI to providers for treatment purposes – for example, information exchanges between a hospital and physicians with admitting privileges at the hospital.

Questions and Answers About Business Associates

Q: Has the Secretary exceeded the statutory authority by requiring "satisfactory assurances" for disclosures to business associates?

A: No. The Health Insurance Portability and Accountability Act of 1996 (HIPAA) gives the Secretary authority to directly regulate health care providers, health plans, and health care clearinghouses. It also grants the Department explicit authority to regulate the uses and disclosures of PHI maintained and transmitted by covered entities. Therefore, we do have the authority to condition the disclosure of PHI by a covered entity to a business associate on the covered entity's having a contract with that business associate.

Q: Has the Secretary exceeded the HIPAA statutory authority by requiring "business associates" to comply with the Privacy Rule, even if that requirement is through a contract?

A: The Privacy Rule does not "pass through" its requirements to business associates or otherwise cause business associates to comply with the terms of the rule. The assurances that covered entities must obtain prior to disclosing PHI to business associates create a set of contractual obligations far narrower than the provisions of the rule, to protect information generally and help the covered entity comply with its obligations under the rule. For example, covered entities do not need to ask their business associates to agree to appoint a privacy officer, or develop policies and procedures for use and disclosure of PHI.

Michael Murphy; Mark Waterfill; Janet Braun

Q: Is it reasonable for covered entities to be held liable for the privacy violations of business associates?

A: A health care provider, health plan, or other covered entity is not liable for privacy violations of a business associate. Covered entities are not required to actively monitor or oversee the means by which the business associate carries out safeguards or the extent to which the business associate abides by the requirements of the contract.

Moreover, a business associate's violation of the terms of the contract does not, in and of itself, constitute a violation of the rule by the covered entity. The contract must obligate the business associate to advise the covered entity when violations have occurred.

If the covered entity becomes aware of a pattern or practice of the business associate that constitutes a material breach or violation of the business associate's obligations under its contract, the covered entity must take "reasonable steps" to cure the breach or to end the violation. Reasonable steps will vary with the circumstances and nature of the business relationship.

If such steps are not successful, the covered entity must terminate the contract if feasible. The rule also provides for circumstances in which termination is not feasible, for example, where there are no other viable business alternatives for the covered entity. In such circumstances where termination is not feasible, the covered entity must report the problem to the Department. Only if the covered entity fails to take the kinds of steps described above would it be considered to be out of compliance with the requirements of the rule.

PARENTS AND MINORS [45 CFR § 164.502(g)]

General Requirements

The Privacy Rule provides individuals with certain rights with respect to their personal health information, including the right to obtain access to and to request amendment of health information about themselves. These rights rest with that individual, or with the "personal representative" of that individual. In general, a person's right to control protected health information (PHI) is based on that person's right (under state or other applicable law, e.g., tribal or military law) to control the health care itself.

Because a parent usually has authority to make health care decisions about his or her minor child, a parent is generally a "personal representative" of his or her minor child under the Privacy Rule and has the right to obtain access to health information about his or her minor child. This would also be true in the case of a guardian or other person acting in loco parentis of a minor.

There are exceptions in which a parent might not be the "personal representative" with respect to certain health information about a minor child. In the following situations, the Privacy Rule defers to determinations under other law that the parent does not control the minor's health care decisions and, thus, does not control the PHI related to that care.

When state or other law does not require consent of a parent or other person before a minor can obtain a particular health care service, and the minor consents to the health care service, the parent is not the minor's personal representative under the Privacy Rule. For example, when a state law provides an adolescent the right to consent to mental health treatment without the consent of his or her parent, and the adolescent obtains such treatment without the consent of the parent, the parent is not the personal representative under the Privacy Rule for that treatment. The minor may choose to involve a parent in these health care decisions without giving up his or her right to control the related health information. Of course, the minor may always have the parent continue to be his or her personal representative even in these situations.

When a court determines or other law authorizes someone other than the parent to make treatment decisions for a minor, the parent is not the personal representative of the minor for the relevant services. For example, courts may grant authority to make health care decisions for the minor to an adult other than the parent, to the minor, or the court may make the decision(s) itself. In order to not undermine these court decisions, the parent is not the personal representative under the Privacy Rule in these circumstances.

In the following situations, the Privacy Rule reflects current professional practice in determining that the parent is not the minor's personal representative with respect to the relevant PHI:

When a parent agrees to a confidential relationship between the minor and the physician, the parent does not have access to the health information related to that conversation or relationship. For example, if a physician asks the parent of a 16-year old if the physician can talk with the child confidentially about a medical condition and the parent agrees, the parent would not control the PHI that was discussed during that confidential conference.

When a physician (or other covered entity) reasonably believes in his or her professional judgment that the child has been or may be subjected to abuse or neglect, or that treating the parent as the child's personal representative could endanger the child, the physician may choose not to treat the parent as the personal representative of the child.

Relation to State Law

In addition to the provisions (described above) tying the right to control information to the right to control treatment, the Privacy Rule also states that it does not preempt state laws that specifically address disclosure of health information about a minor to a parent (§ 160.202). This is true whether the state law authorizes or prohibits such disclosure. Thus, if a physician believes that disclosure of information about a minor would endanger that minor, but a state law requires disclosure to a parent, the physician may comply with the state law without violating the Privacy Rule. Similarly, a provider may comply with a state law that requires disclosure to a parent and would not have to accommodate a request for confidential communications that would be contrary to state law.

Questions and Answers About Parents and Minors

Q: Does the Privacy Rule allow parents the right to see their children's medical records?

A: The Privacy Rule generally allows parents, as their minor children's personal representatives, to have access to information about the health and well being of their children when state or other underlying law allows parents to make treatment decisions for the child. There are two exceptions: (1) when the parent agrees that the minor and the health care provider may have a confidential relationship, the provider is allowed to withhold information from the parent to the extent of that agreement; and (2) when the provider reasonably believes in his or her professional judgment that the child has been or may be subjected to abuse or neglect, or that treating the parent as the child's personal representative could endanger the child, the provider is permitted not to treat the parent as the child's personal representative with respect to health information.

Secretary Thompson has stated that he is reassessing these provisions of the regulation.

Q: Does the Privacy Rule provide rights for children to be treated without parental consent?

A: No. The Privacy Rule does not address consent to treatment, nor does it preempt or change state or other laws that address consent to treatment. The Rule addresses access to health information, not the underlying treatment.

Q: If a child receives emergency medical care without a parent's consent, can the parent get all information about the child's treatment and condition?

A: Generally, yes. Even though the parent did not provide consent to the treatment in this situation, under the Privacy Rule, the parent would still be the child's personal representative. This would not be so only when the minor provided consent (and no other consent is required) or the treating physician suspects abuse or neglect or reasonably believes that releasing the information to the parent will endanger the child.

HEALTH-RELATED COMMUNICATIONS AND MARKETING [45 CFR §§ 164.501, 164.514(e)]

General Requirements

The Privacy Rule addresses the use and disclosure of protected health information (PHI) for marketing purposes in the following ways:

> Defines what is "marketing" under the rule;
> Removes from that definition certain treatment or health care operations activities;
> Set limits on the kind of marketing that can be done as a health care operation; and
> Requires individual authorization for all other uses or disclosures of PHI for marketing purposes.

What Is Marketing

The Privacy Rule defines "marketing" as "a communication about a product or service a purpose of which is to encourage recipients of the communication to purchase or use the product or service." To make this definition easier for covered entities to understand and comply with, we specified what "marketing" is not, as well as generally defined what it is. As questions arise about what activities are "marketing" under the Privacy Rule, we will provide additional clarification regarding such activities.

Communications That Are Not Marketing

The Privacy Rule carves out activities that are not considered marketing under this definition. In recommending treatments or describing available services, health care providers and health plans are advising us to purchase goods and services. To prevent any interference with essential treatment or similar health-related communications with a patient, the rule identifies the following activities as not subject to the marketing provision, even if the activity otherwise meets the definition of marketing. (Written communications for which the covered entity is compensated by a third party are not carved out of the marketing definition.)

Thus, a covered entity is not "marketing" when it:

Describes the participating providers or plans in a network. For example, a health plan is not marketing when it tells its enrollees about which doctors and hospitals are preferred providers, which are included in its network, or which providers offer a particular service. Similarly, a health insurer notifying enrollees of a new pharmacy that has begun to accept its drug coverage is not engaging in marketing.

Describes the services offered by a provider or the benefits covered by a health plan. For example, informing a plan enrollee about drug formulary coverage is not marketing.

Furthermore, it is not marketing for a covered entity to use an individual's PHI to tailor a health-related communication to that individual, when the communication is:

Part of a provider's treatment of the patient and for the purpose of furthering that treatment. For example, recommendations of specific brand name or over-the-counter pharmaceuticals or referrals of patients to other providers are not marketing.

Made in the course of managing the individual's treatment or recommending alternative treatment. For example, reminder notices for appointments, annual exams, or prescription refills are not marketing. Similarly, informing an individual who is a smoker about an effective smoking-cessation program is not marketing, even if that program is offered by someone other than the provider or plan making the recommendation.

Limitations on Marketing Communications

If a communication is marketing, a covered entity may use or disclose PHI to create or make the communication, pursuant to any applicable consent obtained under § 164.506, only in the following circumstances:

It is a face-to-face communication with the individual. For example, sample products may be provided to a patient during an office visit.

It involves products or services of nominal value. For example, a provider can distribute pens, toothbrushes, or key chains with the name of the covered entity or a health care product manufacturer on it.

It concerns the health-related products and services of the covered entity or a third party, and only if the communication:

Identifies the covered entity that is making the communication. Thus, consumers will know the source of these marketing calls or materials.

States that the covered entity is being compensated for making the communication, when that is so.

Tells individuals how to opt out of further marketing communications, with some exceptions as provided in the rule. The covered entity must make reasonable efforts to honor requests to opt-out.

Explains why individuals with specific conditions or characteristics (e.g., diabetics, smokers) have been targeted, if that is so, and how the product or service relates to the health of the individual. The covered entity must also have made a determination that the product or service may be of benefit to individuals with that condition or characteristic.

For all other communications that are "marketing" under the Privacy Rule, the covered entity must obtain the individual's authorization to use or disclose PHI to create or make the marketing communication.

Business Associates (and marketing activities)

Disclosure of PHI for marketing purposes is limited to disclosure to business associates that undertake marketing activities on behalf of the covered entity. No other disclosure for marketing is permitted.

Michael Murphy; Mark Waterfill; Janet Braun

Covered entities may not give away or sell lists of patients or enrollees without obtaining authorization from each person on the list. As with any disclosure to a business associate, the covered entity must obtain the business associate's agreement to use the PHI only for the covered entity's marketing activities. A covered entity may not give PHI to a business associate for the business associate's own purposes.

Questions and Answers About Marketing

Q: Does this rule expand the ability of providers, plans, marketers and others to use my PHI to market goods and services to me?   Does the Privacy Rule make it easier for health care businesses to engage in door-to-door sales and marketing efforts?

A: No. The provisions described above impose limits on the use or disclosure of PHI for marketing that do not exist in most states today. For example, the rule requires patients' authorization for the following types of uses or disclosures of PHI for marketing:

Selling PHI to third parties for their use and re-use. Under the rule, a hospital or other provider may not sell names of pregnant women to baby formula manufacturers or magazines.

Disclosing PHI to outsiders for the outsiders' independent marketing use. Under the rule, doctors may not provide patient lists to pharmaceutical companies for those companies' drug promotions.

These activities can occur today with no authorization from the individual. In addition, for the marketing activities that are allowed by the rule without authorization from the individual, the Privacy Rule requires covered entities to offer individuals the ability to opt-out of further marketing communications.

Similarly, under the business associate provisions of the rule, a covered entity may not give PHI to a telemarketer, door-to-door salesperson, or other marketer it has hired unless that marketer has agreed by contract to use the information only for marketing on behalf of the covered entity. Today, there may be no restrictions on how marketers re-use information they obtain from health plans and providers.

Q: **Can telemarketers gain access to PHI and call individuals to sell goods and services?**

A: Under the rule, unless the covered entity obtains the individual's authorization, it may only give health information to a telemarketer that it has hired to undertake marketing on its behalf. The telemarketer must be a business associate under the rule, which means that it must agree by contract to use the information only for marketing on behalf of the covered entity, and not to market its own goods or services (or those of another third party). The caller must identify the covered entity that is sponsoring the marketing call. The caller must provide individuals the opportunity to opt-out of further marketing.

Q: **When is an authorization required from the patient before a provider or health plan engages in marketing to that individual?**

A: An authorization for use or disclosure of PHI for marketing is always required, unless one of the following three exceptions apply:

The marketing occurs during an in-person meeting with the patient (e.g., during a medical appointment).

The marketing concerns products or services of nominal value.

The covered entity is marketing health-related products and services (of either the covered entity or a third party), the marketing identifies the covered entity that is responsible for the marketing, and the individual is offered an opportunity to opt-out of further marketing. In addition, the marketing must tell people if they have been targeted based on their health status, and must also tell people when the covered entity is compensated (directly or indirectly) for making the communication.

Q: How can I distinguish between activities for treatment, payment or health care operations (TPO) versus marketing activities?

A: There is no need for covered entities to make this distinction. In recommending treatments, providers and health plans advise us to purchase good and services.   The overlap between "treatment," "health care operations," and "marketing" is unavoidable. Instead of creating artificial distinctions, the rule imposes requirements that do not require such distinctions. Specifically:

If the activity is included in the rule's definition of "marketing," the rule's provisions restricting the use or disclosure of PHI for marketing purposes will apply, whether or not that communication also meets the rule's definition of "treatment," "payment," or "health care operations." For these communications, the individual's authorization is required before a covered entity may use or disclose PHI for marketing unless one of the exceptions to the authorization requirement (described above) applies.

The rule exempts certain activities from the definition of "marketing." If an activity falls into one of the definition's exemptions, the marketing rules do not apply. In these cases, covered entities may engage in the activity without first obtaining an authorization if the activity meets the definition of "treatment," "payment," or "health care operations." These exemptions are described above, in the section titled "Communications That Are Not Marketing," and are designed to ensure that nothing in this rule interferes with treatment activities.

Q: Do disease management, health promotion, preventive care, and wellness programs fall under the definition of "marketing"?

A: Whether these kinds of activities fall under the rule's definition of "marketing" depends on the specifics of how the activity is conducted. The activities currently undertaken under these rubrics are diverse. Covered entities must examine the particular activities they undertake, and compare these to the activities that are exempt from the definition of "marketing."

Q: **Can contractors (business associates) use PHI to market to individuals for their own business purposes?**

A: The Privacy Rule prohibits health plans and covered health care providers from giving PHI to third parties for the third party's own business purposes, absent authorization from the individuals. Under the statute, this regulation cannot govern contractors directly.

Michael Murphy; Mark Waterfill; Janet Braun

RESEARCH [45 CFR §§ 164.501, 164.508(f), 164.512(i)]

Background

The Privacy Rule establishes the conditions under which protected health information (PHI) may be used or disclosed by covered entities for research purposes. A covered entity may always use or disclose for research purposes health information which has been de-identified (in accordance with §§ 164.502(d), 164.514(a)-(c) of the rule) without regard to the provisions below.

The Privacy Rule also defines the means by which individuals/human research subjects are informed of how medical information about themselves will be used or disclosed and their rights with regard to gaining access to information about themselves, when such information is held by covered entities. Where research is concerned, the Privacy Rule protects the privacy of individually identifiable health information, while at the same time, ensuring that researchers continue to have access to medical information necessary to conduct vital research. Currently, most research involving human subjects operates under the Common Rule (codified for the Department of Health and Human Services (HHS) at Title 45 Code of Federal Regulations Part 46) and/or the Food and Drug Administration's (FDA) human subjects protection regulations, which have some provisions that are similar to, but more stringent than and separate from, the Privacy Rule's provisions for research.

Using and Disclosing PHI for Research

In the course of conducting research, researchers may create, use, and/or disclose individually identifiable health information. Under the Privacy Rule, covered entities are permitted to use and disclose PHI for research with individual authorization, or without individual authorization under limited circumstances set forth in the Privacy Rule.

Research Use/Disclosure Without Authorization:

To use or disclose PHI without authorization by the research participant, a covered entity must obtain one of the following:

Documentation that an alteration or waiver of research participants' authorization for use/disclosure of information about them for research purposes has been approved by an Institutional Review Board (IRB) or a Privacy Board. This provision of the Privacy Rule might be used, for example, to conduct records research, when researchers are unable to use de-identified information and it is not practicable to obtain research participants' authorization.

or

Representations from the researcher, either in writing or orally, that the use or disclosure of the PHI is solely to prepare a research protocol or for similar purposes preparatory to research, that the researcher will not remove any PHI from the covered entity, and representation that PHI for which access is sought is necessary for the research purpose. This provision might be used, for example, to design a research study or to assess the feasibility of conducting a study.

or

Representations from the researcher, either in writing or orally, that the use or disclosure being sought is solely for research on the PHI of decedents, that the PHI being sought is necessary for the research, and, at the request of the covered entity, documentation of the death of the individuals about whom information is being sought.

A covered entity may use or disclose PHI for research purposes pursuant to a waiver of authorization by an IRB or Privacy Board provided it has obtained documentation of all of the following:

A statement that the alteration or waiver of authorization was approved by an IRB or Privacy Board that was composed as stipulated by the Privacy Rule;

A statement identifying the IRB or Privacy Board and the date on which the alteration or waiver of authorization was approved;

A statement that the IRB or Privacy Board has determined that the alteration or waiver of authorization, in whole or in part, satisfies the following eight criteria:

The use or disclosure of PHI involves no more than minimal risk to the individuals;

The alteration or waiver will not adversely affect the privacy rights and the welfare of the individuals;

The research could not practicably be conducted without the alteration or waiver;

The research could not practicably be conducted without access to and use of the PHI;

The privacy risks to individuals whose PHI is to be used or disclosed are reasonable in relation to the anticipated benefits, if any, to the individuals, and the importance of the knowledge that may reasonably be expected to result from the research;

There is an adequate plan to protect the identifiers from improper use and disclosure;

There is an adequate plan to destroy the identifiers at the earliest opportunity consistent with conduct of the research, unless there is a health or research justification for retaining the identifiers or such retention is otherwise required by law; and

There are adequate written assurances that the PHI will not be reused or disclosed to any other person or entity, except as required by law, for authorized oversight of the research project, or for other research for which the use or disclosure of PHI would be permitted by this subpart.

A brief description of the PHI for which use or access has been determined to be necessary by the IRB or Privacy Board;

A statement that the alteration or waiver of authorization has been reviewed and approved under either normal or expedited review procedures as stipulated by the Privacy Rule; and

The signature of the chair or other member, as designated by the chair, of the IRB or the Privacy Board, as applicable.

Research Use/Disclosure With Individual Authorization:

The Privacy Rule also permits covered entities to use and disclose PHI for research purposes when a research participant authorizes the use or disclosure of information about him or herself. Today, for example, a research participant's authorization will typically be sought for most clinical trials and some records research. In this case, documentation of IRB or Privacy Board approval of a waiver of authorization is not required for the use or disclosure of PHI.

To use or disclose PHI created from a research study that includes treatment (e.g., a clinical trial), additional research-specific elements must be included in the authorization form required under § 164.508, which describe how PHI created for the research study will be used or disclosed. For example, if the covered entity/researcher intends to seek reimbursement from the research subject's health plan for the routine costs of care associated with the protocol, the authorization must describe types of information that will be provided to the health plan. This authorization may be combined with the traditional informed consent document used in research.

The Privacy Rule permits, but does not require, the disclosure of PHI for specified public policy purposes in § 164.512. With few exceptions, the covered entity/researcher may choose to limit its right to disclose information created for a research study that includes treatment to purposes narrower than those permitted by the rule, in accordance with his or her own professional standards.

Questions and Answers About Research

Q: Will the rule hinder medical research by making doctors and others less willing and/or able to share information about individual patients?

A: We do not believe that the Privacy Rule will hinder medical research. Indeed, patients and health plan members should be more willing to participate in research when they know their information is protected. For example, in genetic studies at the National Institutes of Health (NIH), nearly 32 percent of eligible people offered a test for breast cancer risk decline to take it. The overwhelming majority of those who refuse cite concerns about health insurance discrimination and loss of privacy as the reason. The Privacy Rule both permits important research and, at the same time, encourages patients to participate in research by providing much needed assurances about the privacy of their health information.

The Privacy Rule will require some covered health care providers and health plans to change their current practices related to documenting research uses and disclosures. It is possible that some covered health care providers and health plans may conclude that the rule's requirements for research uses and disclosures are too burdensome and will choose to limit researchers' access to PHI. We believe few providers will take this route, however, because the Common Rule includes similar, and more stringent requirements, that have not impaired the willingness of researchers to undertake federally funded research. For example, unlike the Privacy Rule, the Common Rule requires IRB review for all research proposals under its purview, even if informed consent is to be sought. The Privacy Rule requires documentation of IRB or Privacy Board approval only if patient authorization for the use or disclosure of PHI for research purposes is to be altered or waived.

Q: Are some of the criteria so subjective that inconsistent determinations may be made by IRBs and Privacy Boards reviewing similar or identical research projects?

A: Under the Privacy Rule, IRBs and Privacy Boards need to use their judgment as to whether the waiver criteria have been satisfied. Several of the waiver criteria are closely modeled on the Common Rule's criteria for the waiver of informed consent and for the approval of a research study. Thus, it is anticipated that IRBs already have experience in making the necessarily subjective assessments of risks and benefits. While IRBs or Privacy Boards may reach different determinations, the assessment of the waiver criteria through this deliberative process is a crucial element in the current system of safeguarding research participants' privacy. The entire system of local IRBs is, in fact, predicated on a deliberative process that permits local IRB autonomy. The Privacy Rule builds upon this principle; it does not change it.

In addition, for multi-site research that requires PHI from two or more covered entities, the Privacy Rule permits covered entities to accept documentation of IRB or Privacy Board approval from a single IRB or Privacy Board.

Q: Does the Privacy Rule prohibit researchers from conditioning participation in a clinical trial on an authorization to use/disclose existing PHI?

A: No. The Privacy Rule does not address conditions for enrollment in a research study. Therefore, the Privacy Rule in no way prohibits researchers from conditioning enrollment in a research study on the execution of an authorization for the use of pre-existing health information.

Q: Does the Privacy Rule permit the creation of a database for research purposes through an IRB or Privacy Board waiver of individual authorization?

A: Yes. A covered entity may use or disclose PHI without individuals' authorizations for the creation of a research database, provided the covered entity obtains documentation that an IRB or Privacy Board has determined that the specified waiver criteria were satisfied. PHI maintained in such a research database could be used or disclosed for future research studies as permitted by the Privacy Rule – that is, for future studies in which individual authorization has been obtained or where the rule would permit research without an authorization, such as pursuant to an IRB or Privacy Board waiver.

Q: Will IRBs be able to handle the additional responsibilities imposed by the Privacy Rule?

A: Recognizing that some institutions may not have IRBs, or that some IRBs may not have the expertise needed to review research that requires consideration of risks to privacy, the Privacy Rule permits the covered entity to accept documentation of waiver of authorization from an alternative body called a Privacy Board–which could have fewer members, and members with different expertise than IRBs.

In addition, for research that is determined to be of no more than minimal risk, IRBs and Privacy Boards could use an expedited review process, which permits covered entities to accept documentation when only one or more members of the IRB or Privacy Board have conducted the review.

Q: By establishing new waiver criteria and authorization requirements, hasn't the Privacy Rule, in effect, modified the Common Rule?

A: No. Where both the Privacy Rule and the Common Rule apply, both regulations must be followed. The Privacy Rule regulates only the content and conditions of the documentation that covered entities must obtain before using or disclosing PHI for research purposes.

Q: Is documentation of IRB and Privacy Board approval required before a covered entity would be permitted to disclose PHI for research purposes without an individual's authorization?

A: No. The Privacy Rule requires documentation of waiver approval by either an IRB or a Privacy Board, not both.

Q: Does a covered entity need to create an IRB or Privacy Board before using or disclosing PHI for research?

A: No. The IRB or Privacy Board could be created by the covered entity or the recipient researcher, or it could be an independent board.

Q: What does the Privacy Rule say about a research participant's right of access to research records or results?

A: With few exceptions, the Privacy Rule gives patients the right to inspect and obtain a copy of health information about themselves that is maintained in a "designated record set." A designated record set is basically a group of records which a covered entity uses to make decisions about individuals, and includes a health care provider's medical records and billing records, and a health plan's enrollment, payment, claims adjudication, and case or medical management record systems.   Research records or results maintained in a designated record set are accessible to research participants unless one of the Privacy Rule's permitted exceptions applies.

One of the permitted exceptions applies to PHI created or obtained by a covered health care provider/researcher for a clinical trial. The Privacy Rule permits the individual's access rights in these cases to be suspended while the clinical trial is in progress, provided the research participant agreed to this denial of access when consenting to participate in the clinical trial.   In addition, the health care provider/researcher must inform the research participant that the right to access PHI will be reinstated at the conclusion of the clinical trial.

Q: Are the Privacy Rule's requirements regarding patient access in harmony with the Clinical Laboratory Improvements Amendments of 1988 (CLIA)?

A: Yes. The Privacy Rule does not require clinical laboratories that are also covered health care providers to provide an individual access to information if CLIA prohibits them from doing so. CLIA permits clinical laboratories to provide clinical laboratory test records and reports only to "authorized persons," as defined primarily by state law. The individual who is the subject of the information is not

Michael Murphy; Mark Waterfill; Janet Braun

always included as an authorized person. Therefore, the Privacy Rule includes an exception to individuals' general right to access PHI about themselves if providing an individual such access would be in conflict with CLIA.

In addition, for certain research laboratories that are exempt from the CLIA regulations, the Privacy Rule does not require such research laboratories if they are also a covered health care provider to provide individuals with access to PHI because doing so may result in the research laboratory losing its CLIA exemption.

Q: Do the Privacy Rule's requirements for authorization and the Common Rule's requirements for informed consent differ?

A: Yes. Under the Privacy Rule, a patient's authorization will be used for the use and disclosure of PHI for research purposes. In contrast, an individual's informed consent as required by the Common Rule and FDA's human subjects regulations is a consent to participate in the research study as a whole, not simply a consent for the research use or disclosure of PHI. For this reason, there are important differences between the Privacy Rule's requirements for individual authorization, and the Common Rule's and FDA's requirements for informed consent. Where the Privacy Rule, the Common Rule, and/or FDA's human subjects regulations are applicable, each of the applicable regulations will need to be followed.

RESTRICTIONS ON GOVERNMENT ACCESS TO HEALTH INFORMATION [45 CFR §§ 160.300; 164.512(b); 164.512(f)]

Background

Under the Privacy Rule, government-operated health plans and health care providers must meet substantially the same requirements as private ones for protecting the privacy of individual identifiable health information. For instance, government-run health plans, such as Medicare and Medicaid, must take virtually the same steps to protect the claims and health information that they receive from beneficiaries as private insurance plans or health maintenance organizations (HMO). In addition, all federal agencies must also meet the requirements of the Privacy Act of 1974, which restricts what information about individual citizens – including any personal health information – can be shared with other agencies and with the public.

The only new authority for government involves enforcement of the Privacy Rule itself. In order to ensure covered entities protect patients' privacy as required, the rule provides that health plans, hospitals, and other covered entities cooperate with the Department's efforts to investigate complaints or otherwise ensure compliance. The Department of Health and Human Services (HHS) Office for Civil Rights (OCR) is responsible for enforcing the privacy protections and access rights for consumers under this rule.

Questions and Answers About Government Access To Private Health Care Information

Q: Does the rule require my doctor to send my medical records to the government?

A: No. The rule does not require a physician or any other covered entity to send medical information to the government for a government data base or similar operation. This rule does not require or allow any new government access to medical information, with one exception: the rule does give OCR the authority to investigate complaints and to otherwise ensure that covered entities comply with the rule.

OCR has been assigned the responsibility of enforcing the Privacy Rule. As is typical in many enforcement settings, OCR may need to look at how a covered entity handled medical records and other personal health information. The Privacy Rule limits disclosure to OCR to information that is "pertinent to ascertaining compliance." OCR will maintain stringent controls to safeguard any individually identifiable health information that it receives. If covered entities could avoid or ignore enforcement requests, consumers would not have a way to ensure an independent review of their concerns about privacy violations under the rule.

Q: Why would a Privacy Rule require covered entities to turn over anybody's personal health information as part of a government enforcement process?

A: An important ingredient in ensuring compliance with the Privacy Rule is the Department's responsibility to investigate complaints that the rule has been violated and to follow up on other information regarding noncompliance. At times, this responsibility entails seeing personal health information, such as when an individual indicates to the Department that they believe a covered entity has not properly handled their medical records.

What information would be needed depends on the circumstances and the alleged violations. The Privacy Rule limits OCR's access to information that is "pertinent to ascertaining compliance." In some cases, no personal health information would be needed. For instance, OCR may need to review only a business contract to determine whether a health plan included appropriate language to protect privacy when it hired an outside company to help process claims.

Examples of investigations that may require OCR to have access to protected health information (PHI) include:

Allegations that a covered entity refused to note a request for correction in a patient's medical record, or did not provide complete access to a patient's medical records to that patient.

Allegations that a covered entity used health information for marketing purposes without first obtaining the individuals' authorization when required by the rule. OCR may need to review information in the marketing department that contains personal health information, to determine whether a violation has occurred.

Q: Will this rule make it easier for police and law enforcement agencies to get my medical information?

A: No. The rule does not expand current law enforcement access to individually identifiable health information. In fact, it limits access to a greater degree than currently exists. Today, law enforcement officers obtain health information for many purposes, sometimes without a warrant or other prior process. The rule establishes new procedures and safeguards to restrict the circumstances under which a covered entity may give such information to law enforcement officers.

For example, the rule limits the type of information that covered entities may disclose to law enforcement, absent a warrant or other prior process, when law enforcement is seeking to identify or locate a suspect. It specifically prohibits disclosure of DNA information for this purpose, absent some other legal requirements such as a warrant. Similarly, under most circumstances, the Privacy Rule requires covered entities to obtain permission from persons who have been the victim of domestic violence or abuse before disclosing information about them to law enforcement. In most states, such permission is not required today.

Where state law imposes additional restrictions on disclosure of health information to law enforcement, those state laws continue to apply. This rule sets a national floor of legal protections; it is not a set of "best practices."

Even in those circumstances when disclosure to law enforcement is permitted by the rule, the Privacy Rule does not require covered entities to disclose any information. Some other federal or state law may require a disclosure, and the Privacy Rule does not interfere with the operation of these other laws. However, unless the disclosure is required by some other law, covered entities should use their professional judgment to decide whether to disclose information, reflecting their own policies and ethical principles. In other words, doctors, hospitals, and health plans could continue to follow their own policies to protect privacy in such instances.

Q: Must a health care provider or other covered entity obtain permission from a patient prior to notifying public health authorities of the occurrence of a reportable disease?

A: No. All states have laws that require providers to report cases of specific diseases to public health officials. The Privacy Rule allows disclosures that are required by law. Furthermore, disclosures to public health authorities that are authorized by law to collect or receive information for public health purposes are also permissible under the Privacy Rule. In order to do their job of protecting the health of the public, it is frequently necessary for public health officials to obtain information about the persons affected by a disease. In some cases they may need to contact those affected in order to determine the cause of the disease to allow for actions to prevent further illness.

The Privacy Rule continues to allow for the existing practice of sharing PHI with public health authorities that are authorized by law to collect or receive such information to aid them in their mission of protecting the health of the public. Examples of such activities include those directed at the reporting of disease or injury, reporting deaths and births, investigating the occurrence and cause of injury and disease, and monitoring adverse outcomes related to food, drugs, biological products, and dietary supplements.

Q: How does the rule affect my rights under the federal Privacy Act?

A: The Privacy Act of 1974 protects personal information about individuals held by the federal government. Covered entities that are federal agencies or federal contractors that maintain records that are covered by the Privacy Act not only must obey the Privacy Rule's requirements but also must comply with the Privacy Act.

PAYMENT [45 CFR 164.501]

General Requirements

As provided for by the Privacy Rule, a covered entity may use and disclose protected health information (PHI) for payment purposes. "Payment" is a defined term that encompasses the various activities of health care providers to obtain payment or be reimbursed for their services and for a health plan to obtain premiums, to fulfill their coverage responsibilities and provide benefits under the plan, and to obtain or provide reimbursement for the provision of health care.

In addition to the general definition, the Privacy Rule provides examples of common payment activities which include, but are not limited to:

Determining eligibility or coverage under a plan and adjudicating claims;
Risk adjustments;
Billing and collection activities;
Reviewing health care services for medical necessity, coverage, justification of charges, and the like;
Utilization review activities; and
Disclosures to consumer reporting agencies (limited to specified identifying information about the individual, his or her payment history, and identifying information about the covered entity).

Questions and Answers About Payment

Q: Does the rule prevent reporting to consumer credit reporting agencies or otherwise create any conflict with the Fair Credit Reporting Act (FCRA)?

A: No. The Privacy Rule's definition of "payment" includes disclosures to consumer reporting agencies.   These disclosures, however, are limited to the following PHI about the individual: name and address; date of birth; social security number; payment history; account number. In addition, disclosure of the name and address of the health care provider or health plan making the report is allowed. The covered entity may perform this payment activity directly or may carry out this function through a third party, such as a collection agency, under a business associate arrangement.

We are not aware of any conflict in the consumer credit reporting disclosures permitted by the Privacy Rule and FCRA. The Privacy Rule permits uses and disclosures by the covered entity or its business associate as may be required by FCRA or other law.   Therefore, we do not believe there would be a conflict between the Privacy Rule and legal duties imposed on data furnishers by FCRA.

Q: Does the Privacy Rule prevent health plans and providers from using debt collection agencies? Does the rule conflict with the Fair Debt Collection Practices Act?

A: The Privacy Rule permits covered entities to continue to use the services of debt collection agencies. Debt collection is recognized as a payment activity within the "payment" definition. Through a business associate arrangement, the covered entity may engage a debt collection agency to perform this function on its behalf. Disclosures to collection agencies under a business associate agreement are governed by other provisions of the rule, including consent (where consent is required) and the minimum necessary requirements.

We are not aware of any conflict between the Privacy Rule and the Fair Debt Collection Practices Act. Where a use or disclosure of PHI is necessary for the covered entity to fulfill a legal duty, the Privacy Rule would permit such use or disclosure as required by law.

Q: Are location information services of collection agencies, which are required under the Fair Debt Collection Practices Act, permitted under the Privacy Rule?

A: "Payment" is broadly defined as activities by health plans or health care providers to obtain premiums or obtain or provide reimbursements for the provision of health care. The activities specified are by way of example and are not intended to be an exclusive listing. Billing, claims management, collection activities and related data processing are expressly included in the definition of "payment." Obtaining information about the location of the individual is a routine activity to facilitate the collection of amounts owed and the management of accounts receivable, and, therefore, would constitute a payment activity. The covered entity and its business associate would also have to comply with any limitations placed on location information services by the Fair Debt Collection Practices Act., with civil and criminal penalties that can be imposed if they violate patients' privacy rights.

And it strikes a balance when public responsibility requires disclosure of some forms of data – for example, to protect public health.

For patients – it means being able to make informed choices when seeking care and reimbursement for care based on how personal health information may be used.

It enables patients to find out how their information may be used and what disclosures of their information have been made.
It generally limits release of information to the minimum reasonably needed for the purpose of the disclosure.

Michael Murphy; Mark Waterfill; Janet Braun

It gives patients the right to examine and obtain a copy of their own health records and request corrections.

Index Of Key Terms

Term

Access, 63, 70, 133
Accounting, 33, 34, 63
ADA, 49, 52, 62, 66, 144
Administrative, 33, 37, 63, 70, 73, 84, 86
Authorization, 5, 12, 26, 27, 28, 49, 75, 125, 127
Business Associates, 9, 70, 72, 75, 111, 119
Certification, 51, 144
Complaints, 31
Compliance, iii, 1, 7, 33, 35, 37, 45, 49, 50, 143, 144
Consent, 5, 13, 19, 21, 83, 84, 86, 87
Contact Person, 36, 48
Covered Entities, 12, 31
Disclosure, 15, 26, 47, 72, 119, 125, 127
Documentation, 29, 34, 35, 47, 125
FMLA, 49, 52, 144
Health Care Operations, 12
Health Plans, 7, 12, 14, 25
HHS, 3, 4, 6, 7, 11, 33, 44, 46, 48, 61, 78, 82, 83, 84, 96, 124, 133
HIPAA, iii, 1, 2, 3, 4, 6, 7, 11, 12, 15, 17, 19, 32, 35, 36, 38, 39, 40, 45, 46, 48, 50, 52, 53, 54, 58, 65, 66, 67, 69, 73, 75, 76, 80, 82, 96, 111, 143, 144
Job Descriptions, 48
Mitigation, 31, 69
OSHA, 26, 49, 143, 144
Payment, 12, 14, 15, 137, 138, 139
Penalties, 31, 47
Personal Representative, 17, 59
PHI, 4, 5, 6, 11, 12, 13, 15, 16, 17, 19, 20, 21, 22, 23, 24, 25, 26, 29, 31, 33, 34, 35, 36, 37, 38, 40, 43, 44, 45, 46, 47, 48, 49, 50, 51, 52, 53, 54, 62, 63, 64, 66, 67, 69, 70, 71, 72, 73, 75, 76, 77, 85, 86, 87, 88, 89, 90, 91, 92, 93, 94, 95, 96, 97, 98, 99, 102, 104, 105, 107, 108, 110, 111, 113, 114, 117, 118, 119, 120, 121, 122, 123, 124, 125, 126, 127, 128, 129, 130, 131, 132, 134, 136, 137, 138, 139
Pre-HIPAA, 2
Privacy Notice, 38, 47, 49, 55
Privacy Officer, 36, 48, 53, 55, 61, 62, 66, 70, 71, 72, 73, 74, 75, 77
Privacy Policy, 31, 52

Michael Murphy; Mark Waterfill; Janet Braun

Privacy Rule, 3, 4, 5, 6, 7, 9,
    10, 11, 12, 15, 17, 19, 20,
    22, 23, 24, 25, 31, 32, 33,
    35, 36, 39, 40, 41, 42, 43,
    44, 45, 46, 47, 48, 49, 50,
    52, 53, 58, 61, 65, 66, 67,
    69, 73, 75, 76, 78, 79, 80,
    81, 82, 83, 84, 85, 86, 87,
    88, 89, 90, 91, 92, 93, 94,
    95, 96, 97, 98, 99, 100, 101,
    102, 103, 104, 105, 106,
    107, 108, 109, 110, 111,
    112, 113, 114, 115, 116,
    117, 119, 120, 123, 124,
    125, 126, 127, 128, 129,
    130, 131, 132, 133, 134,
    135, 136, 137, 138, 139

Providers, 12, 42, 101, 104,
    108
Retaliation, 32, 47, 61
Safeguards, 70
Security, 15, 48, 54, 56, 63,
    101
TPO, 12, 13, 19, 20, 21, 22,
    24, 49, 85, 86, 87, 88, 89,
    90, 91, 92, 94, 95, 109, 122
Training, iii, 36, 48, 49, 64, 69,
    81, 143, 144
Transactions, 16, 42, 101
Treatment, 12, 98
Use, 26, 50, 63, 72, 73, 125,
    127
Waivers, 48

About the Author

Michael Murphy, SPHR
M.S. I/O Psychology

Areas of Concentration: Human Resources Management Consulting; Writing; Training; Public Speaking; Seminars; Workshops; Conferences: and serving as an Expert Witness in HR related matters.

Education: University of Indianapolis, with a B.A. in Psychology. Masters of Science In Industrial/Organizational Psychology from Purdue University at Indianapolis. Accepted in the American Psychological Association and the Society for Industrial/Organizational Psychology.

Experience: Mr. Murphy is the founder and president of Premier Consulting Services Inc. **PCS***i*® is a Human Resources Consulting Firm providing services to clients across the United States. Mike is a nationally recognized author, speaker and seminar leader. He has been the principle speaker at seminars and workshops held in such diverse locations as Halifax Nova Scotia, Cancun Mexico, Maui, Hawaii, and St. Thomas the US Virgin Islands. As a speaker Mr. Murphy has traveled the United States presenting training seminars, conferences and workshops. Mr. Murphy has authored numerous books on issues related to human resources management. Recently Mike, along with Attorney Mark Waterfill has authored OSHA Reporting Requirements And Revised Record Keeping 2002: A Compliance Guide, and has served as Editor of The Employer's Guide To Worker's Compensation In Indiana.

In addition to his speaking, writing and consulting, duties Mike provides Expert Witness services in all areas of HR Management and has served as an Expert Witness in cases involving sexual harassment, race discrimination, age discrimination, disability discrimination, and unfair labor practices. We are sure you will find **Understanding HIPAA, a Compliance Guide For Employers** informative, well written, and most importantly, useful.

Janet Braun, SPHR, BA, Paralegal

Areas of Concentration: Human Resources Management Consulting; Benefits Management; Compliance; Training; and Employee Development.

Education: Bachelor of Arts – Paralegal, St. Mary of the Woods College, Terre Haute Indiana. Certified as a Senior Professional In Human Resources Management, SPHR by the Human Resources Certification Institute.

Experience: Since earning her degree over ten years ago, Janet has worked exclusively in the field of Human Resources rising from an Employment Specialist to a Generalist level in her knowledge and experience in HR matters. Currently, Janet is a Senior Accounts Manager with Premier Consulting Services Inc., providing Human Resources – Personnel consulting services to clients across the United States. In her capacity as a Senior Account Manager, Janet provides HR consulting services to clients and she also supervises other consultants providing services for PCSi. Her area of specialty is on-site – out sourced Human Resources intervention services. In that capacity Janet has assisted clients with compliance in FMLA; ADA; OSHA; IRCA; Title VII; ADEA; and Worker's Compensation issues. Janet's training, experience and education as a paralegal are valuable assets in these areas. Because of her training as a paralegal Janet is uniquely qualified to work with client's legal counsel addressing complex compliance issues. In addition to her consulting duties Janet also participates as a speaker in PCSi sponsored seminars at both "on-site" and public seminars, speaking on compliance related issues. Janet is an author and together with Mike Murphy and Mark Waterfill has served as co-author and editor of <u>The Employer's Guide To Worker's Compensation In Indiana</u>, and <u>Understanding HIPAA, A Compliance Guide For Employers.</u>

Mark R. Waterfill
Attorney-at-Law
Dann Pecar Newman & Kleiman, P.C.
Shareholder
317.632.3232 ext. 119
mwaterfill@dannpecar.com
PRACTICE AREAS:
Employment Law and Commercial
Litigation.

EDUCATION:
Hanover College, Indiana, B.S., *magna cum laude,* 1983; Indiana University School of Law at Bloomington, J.D., 1986.

EXPERIENCE:
As an Attorney concentrating his practice on Employment Law and Commercial Litigation, Mr. Waterfill has handled first chair responsibility in several complex litigation matters ranging from class-action overtime and age discrimination cases to securities fraud and breach of contract matters. Mr. Waterfill has also litigated and successfully argued before the Indiana Court of Appeals on covenants not to compete issues.

In addition to his law practice, Mark is a frequent lecturer on various topics related to employment law, as well as a litigation partner focusing on commercial disputes. Mr. Waterfill has spoken on diverse topics such as religious discrimination in employment, arbitration and mediation of employment disputes, how to fire employees and various other employment law issues. Below is a partial list of Mark's most recent seminars.

- Understanding Employment Law from Application To Termination, Indianapolis Indiana, May 2003
- Avoiding Legal Problems: The Overlap between FMLA, ADA, and Worker's Compensation, Indianapolis, Indiana, April 2003
- Personnel Law Update: Law and Psychology of The Workplace, Indianapolis, Indiana March, 2003

MEMBERSHIPS : Indianapolis Bar Association; Indiana Bar Association; American Bar Association

Printed in the United States
36110LVS00004B/69

9 781410 788788